OXFORD MUSIC EXAMINATION WORKBOOKS

Anna Butterworth

Stylistic Harmony

WORK BOOK
Second Edition

OXFORD UNIVERSITY PRESS
Oxford and New York

To Professor Ivor Keys

Acknowledgements

I should like to thank my colleague Philip Sawyer, at Napier University, Edinburgh, for his help and advice, and to express my deep gratitude to Pamela Brydon for her assistance in the preparation of the final manuscript. Many thanks go also to my husband, Neil, for his valuable proof-reading, and to Mrs Carol Crawford for patiently typing a complex manuscript with such care.

A.B.

Oxford University Press, Great Clarendon Street, Oxford OX2 6DP
Oxford New York
Athens Auckland Bangkok Bogota Bombay
Buenos Aires Calcutta Cape Town Dar es Salaam
Delhi Florence Hong Kong Istanbul Karachi
Kuala Lumpur Madras Madrid Melbourne
Mexico City Nairobi Paris Singapore
Taipei Tokyo Toronto
and associated companies in
Berlin Ibadan

Oxford is a trade mark of Oxford University Press

First edition © Oxford University Press 1992.   Second edition © Oxford University Press 1994.
Reprinted 1996, 1997

First edition first published 1992. Reprinted 1993 (twice)
Second edition first published 1994

British Library Cataloguing in Publication Data
Data available

ISBN 0 19 321059 2

Designed by Fran Holdsworth

Printed in Hong Kong

Preface

This book outlines the main features of musical style between 1550 and 1850. The product of many years of teaching experience has been gathered into book form in response to the relatively recent demand of most bodies examining in music for GCE 'A' level, for entrance to University or (Music) College, or for Diplomas, that the student be able to demonstrate a knowledge and understanding of a variety of harmonic styles. It is therefore suitable for use with sixth-formers, students at Colleges of Further Education (for whom it was originally written), and others preparing for such examinations.

As this book was designed to provide systematic exposure to the styles covered in examination syllabuses, it is presented as a chronological course of study, with, at every stage, examples and exercises sufficient for a two-year course. Teachers may none the less prefer to dip into certain sections in conjunction with their own harmony courses. Greatest weight has been given to those chapters dealing with the Baroque and Classical periods, since these are basic areas of harmonic technique and experience. It is recommended, however, that a study of counterpoint begin with the Renaissance, where the principles of imitation and dissonance, for example, may be appreciated from their beginnings.

Of paramount importance in the development of a feel for stylistic harmony is the aural aspect; this can, and should, be fostered just as rigorously in the classroom as in private tuition. Initial bad teaching frequently results in a student having little or no perception of the sounds he writes or reads off the page, and with no inkling of the necessity for this skill. All examples marked ❏ should therefore be sung or played before working, or used as aural exercises. Whilst the other exercises may be attempted away from an instrument, students should always check their work at the keyboard on completion, in order to correct anything mis'heard'; this will help the ear to develop. The student who has worked at harmony in a vacuum and found it a pointless drudgery beset with rules, can come to realize instead that it is a vital component of the music he sings, plays, and hears, provided that harmony is sympathetically integrated with other aspects of musical study, such as aural perception, history, and form. Thus it is hoped that an attractive example or exercise in this book may stimulate further listening, perhaps of the complete work, and raise comment and discussion to the satisfaction of student and teacher alike. Through deeper understanding of a composer's language of communication (his technique and style), the student can be helped both to perform more sensitively, and to gain greater enjoyment from his listening.

The workbook format adopted for *Stylistic Harmony* should eliminate for the student the tedious and time-consuming chore of copying exercises from text or blackboard; simultaneously it provides a lasting work of reference.

Please note that the student is referred to as 'he' for ease of text only.

Over the past thirty years of teaching I have been indebted to the authors of several harmony books, and I apologize if I have unwittingly used any of their ideas or material.

Anna Butterworth

Note to the second edition 1994

The second edition includes corrections and revisions which have been incorporated into the second edition of Stylistic Harmony Answer Book. The answers in the answer book are printed in small type.

Contents

Introduction

The 'Hearing' Problem

For many students the working of harmony exercises has been carried out solely by the application of rules taught in harmony manuals. Many students will admit that it was never suggested that they should actually try to 'hear' what they wrote; playing through worked exercises was discouraged or even forbidden, on the grounds that an instrument would not be available in the examination room. Yet the ability to 'hear' is essential for any serious musician, a skill required not only for the working of harmony and counterpoint but also in composition, and in the reading and learning of scores away from the keyboard. The aural aspect is therefore well worth the trouble for what may seem slow progress; some suggestions for its development are included below.

Labelling Chords

It has to be admitted, none the less, that for many students the difficulty of 'hearing' is such that the teacher is tempted to give up, and resort to teaching harmony by numbers and rules rather than persevere with the development of aural memory. Even with assiduous aural training the student may still feel insecure. Luckily, however, there are many clues and signposts to help the ear and, in the end, successful working of an exercise depends not only on what is heard, but also on an awareness of the idioms of that particular style of composition.

In the past harmony textbooks have tended to overstress the importance of abstract rules, ignoring the fact that harmonic style cannot be divorced from the period in which the music was written: specific 'rules' belong to certain eras; they are simply the 'style in action'. For instance, such texts usually warn students never, in part-writing, to double the 3rd of the major triad, yet Bach (e.g. in his chorales) frequently does this very thing (see Chapter 3). The point is that in the Bachian context the doubled 3rd — which can sound oversweet — is generally the outcome of two strong parts moving by step in contrary motion, neither involving a note or interval which might require special treatment. Thus certain formulae are not intrinsically 'right' or 'wrong' but simply characteristic, or otherwise, of their day. Students should therefore be encouraged always to analyse and label the music they are studying or writing, in order to take effective note of the formulae, intervals, and progressions which characterized each period.

Figured bass (whose working is explained in Chapter 2) is so important in Baroque music that it is used throughout this book whenever musical shorthand is required; it is of particular value in describing chromatic harmony. However, figured bass by itself gives no indication of chords and their progressions and, in my own teaching, I have found it imperative that the student be able to identify each triad and its position (e.g. I, iib, V⁷d) in order to appreciate fully its function in the music. Therefore, when writing about chords I have tended to follow the tradition of earlier OUP publications and use Ib, Ic, V⁷d, etc., rather than adopt the system current in many American harmony texts of combining these labellings and so identifying such chords as I⁶, I⁶₄ , V⁴₃. I believe that students should be fluent in both labellings and that the 'American' version is clear and concise on paper, but my personal experience is that in oral discussion it is confusing for the less mature student, tending to sound like a variety of telephone numbers. Teachers are invited to consider these issues carefully, so that whichever method is adopted becomes part of a systematic approach which the student employs habitually until such time as those props are no longer required.

The following system of identifying keys and triads will be used throughout this book; each chord symbol accurately reflects the sound of the chord, which the student will learn to recognize. The keys given indicate the key at the *beginning* of an extract.

Major keys are indicated by capital (upper-case) letters, e.g. C = C major.

Minor keys are indicated by small (lower-case) letters, e.g. c = C minor.

Large roman numerals are used for major and augmented triads.

Small roman numerals are used for minor and diminished triads.

An accidental before a chord symbol alters the root of that chord.

An accidental before a figure alters that interval.

The diminished 5th of a triad is indicated by °, the augmented 5th by +.

The diminished 7th chord is labelled ᵈ⁷.

The augmented 6th labelling may be abbreviated to Aug. 6 (It.), Aug. 6 (Ger.), Aug. 6 (Fr.).

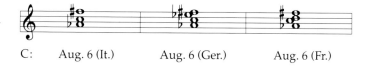

Here are some examples of altered chords:

Chord I

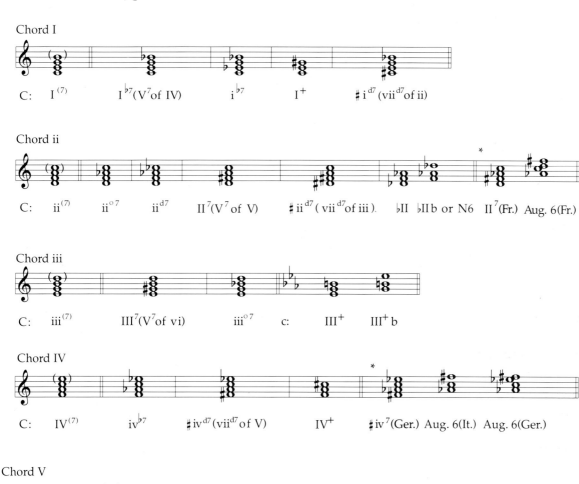

C: I$^{(7)}$ I^{b7}(V^{7}of IV)   i^{b7} I$^+$ $\sharp$i^{d7}(vii^{d7}of ii)

Chord ii

C: ii$^{(7)}$ ii^{o7} ii^{d7} II^7(V^{7}of V) $\sharp$ii^{d7}(vii^{d7}of iii) $\flat$II $\flat$IIb or N6 II^7(Fr.) Aug. 6(Fr.)

Chord iii

C: iii$^{(7)}$ III^7(V^{7}of vi)   iii^{o7} c: III$^+$ III$^+$b

Chord IV

C: IV$^{(7)}$ iv^{b7} $\sharp$iv^{d7}(vii^{d7}of V)   IV$^+$ $\sharp$iv^7(Ger.) Aug. 6(It.) Aug. 6(Ger.)

Chord V

C: V$^{(7)}$ v$^{(7)}$ V$^+$ $\sharp$v^{d7}(vii^{d7}of vi)

Chord vi

C: vi^7 VI^7(V^{7}of ii) $\flat$VI $\flat$VI^7(V^{7}of $\flat$II)

Chord vii

C: vii$^{(7)}$ vii^{d7} VII^7(V^{7}of iii) $\flat$VII

* Triad neither major nor minor

General Hints on Aural Development

The formation of chords must be learned by the student through ear, eye and hand.

The Juilliard Report on *Teaching the Literature and Materials of Music* (New York, 1953)

1. The student *must* be able to sing the given melody or bass; how else can he 'hear' the harmony implied? This is only possible if he has acquired a reasonable facility in *sight-singing*. Ample easy practice material is available in hymn-books, folk-song collections, etc. In this direction self-improvement is clearly possible. In class the sight-reading of chorales, songs, and easy choruses in parts is very helpful.

2. The frequent following of scores is useful: (*a*) since the notation is allied to the sound it is 'rudiments in action'; (*b*) the eye may well help the ear to hear more detail in the music; and (*c*) the 'look' of a score may be enough to place it in a historical context, e.g. a Handel fugue will appear very different from a Strauss tone-poem.

3. Frequent reference to particular progressions, such as suspensions or cadences, should be made when the student is actually *playing* or *singing* them; no instrumental lesson or choir rehearsal should pass without such references, and, particularly when the music is making an effective point, the student should be helped to understand how this is done. In this way he can appreciate and *memorize* the sound and its effect in a musical context.

4. Students should be encouraged to copy out their favourite passages as examples of progressions and be able to play and/or sing them.

5. In class it is helpful to sing in two parts — soprano and bass, if possible. (See the figured chorales in two parts in A. Riemenschneider, *371 Harmonized Chorales*.) In this way the 'bare bones' of the harmonic structure are emphasized and the importance of the bass part appreciated. Students may also be encouraged to improvise bass parts to melodies, starting with tunes they know.

6. The cadence progressions are the easiest to grasp and retain by the ear, starting with V–I and gradually extending the formula by working backwards to iib–V–I, then vi or Ib–iib–V–I. Frequent repetition of these formulae — always using familiar material, such as the National Anthem, folksongs, carols, or the latest pop song— should help to imprint the sound with its 'label' on the memory, especially if the examples are worked aurally on paper *and* played *and* sung. Much harmony can be worked backwards from the cadence anyway, by opting for the strong progressions. Other 'stock' progressions or chords (such as passing $^6_4$s and $^6_3$s and suspensions) may be absorbed in the same way in the stylistic context, initial reference and identification always being made with familiar material.[1]

7. Another helpful exercise is the writing down from memory of a familiar tune, such as a carol. This is a good test of rudiments — notation, intervals, etc. The student should then attempt to add the harmony he 'hears'. He should always check his

---

[1] Other textbooks which acknowledge the importance of teaching harmonic awareness through already familiar material, and encourage students to play or sing examples and exercises, include *The Oxford Students' Harmony* by E. Smith and D. Renouf (OUP, 1965) and *Harmony and Style* by N. Long (Faber, 1968).

results at the piano and note the errors, to discover where and why his ear 'went wrong'. Whenever possible the teacher should not obliterate a student's mistakes with the correction but retain both versions so that they can be played and compared.

8. An invaluable source of harmonic material lies in chorale and hymn-books, and students should be urged to dip into these at the keyboard on a regular basis. Weaker performers will gain pianistically, and all will benefit from playing the same formulae in many varied and beautiful guises. Again, repetition of strong harmonic progressions will help commit their sound to memory. In this respect Anglican chants, often 'pearls of great price', are very useful in that the progressions are repeated many times in their performance.

Some Guidelines on the Working of Exercises

The exercise to be worked must be 'sung through' in the head. The key (major or minor) in which it begins is indicated by a letter under the key signature; once this and the melody (or bass-line) are grasped — the first important step — the student may well 'hear' a harmonization in his head. He should establish the following points as a result of what he has 'heard'; the rest is detective work and the application of formulae according to the style of the music.

1. Establish the type of piece. This, along with the tempo indication, may determine the harmonic rhythm (i.e. the number of chords per bar). For example, a chorale will probably imply more changes of harmony than a Haydn string quartet passage. Look for other possible stylistic features of the piece: e.g. in a binary composition the opening and closing bars of each section may well be the same, or very similar, given the key differences; this should be noted in the harmonization.

2. If the opening has been worked, then the given style should be maintained and the given material used and developed. Any new ideas or figurations introduced should be used at least twice, so as not to sound haphazard.

3. Modulations, which hopefully will have been 'heard' in the sing-through, should be noted; accidentals provide clues. It is helpful to make a note of the closely-related keys at the outset, so that one is aware of the most likely modulations.

4. Note and label the cadences. Phrase marks may determine these: i.e. a phrase ending should indicate a cadence. If there is no phrasing, then the normal phrase lengths of two and four bars will probably apply.

5. Look for any evidence of the use of dissonance. Clues include: (a) notes tied or repeated over the barline, or from a weak to a strong beat, then moving down by step — this will probably indicate a suspension (mark with an 'S'); (b) two notes slurred together — where the first may be an accented passing note or an appoggiatura, and will therefore be dissonant (there will probably be only one chord under two slurred notes).

6. The given part may suggest contrapuntal treatment in the form of imitation, in the use of figurations, or in the appearance of sequences. (Mark in any of these.)

7. The remaining chords should be indicated and the outside parts filled in and

checked for consecutives. Movement in contrary motion is always strong.

8. The inside parts (if any) should be added, and the whole checked for consecutives, accidentals, and phrasing.

It is important for students always to indicate the chords they are using; any weak progressions they may write, such as ii–I (post-Renaissance style), will then be 'staring them in the face', while the strong progressions, such as vi–iib–V–I, will follow the formula they know 'works', which, with practice, they will hopefully come to hear.

In class, teachers may find it helpful to 'talk-through' exercises, including the points above which are relevant, so that the student learns *always* to use a systematic approach.

1. The Renaissance Period
(c.1475–1600)

The great era of the Renaissance saw the rebirth of humanism in a new light—one in which the artist emerged as an individual with his own personal way of using the accepted style. Bound up for a while with mathematical principles, music lagged behind the other arts in some respects until Josquin des Prez (1440–1521), described by Martin Luther as 'the master of the notes', emerged as the first outstanding Renaissance composer. Josquin's aim was to enhance, through sound, the meaning and mood of the text (most music of the time being allied to text), and he consequently earned the title of 'the painter'. Such expressive and emotional aims, seen as the essence of late Renaissance style, resulted in a mode of composition known thereafter as 'musica reservata'.

The single most important expression of the Renaissance spirit may be seen in the Protestant Reformation, a movement which was primarily concerned with the freedom of the individual and his personal relationship with his God. Luther made his stand against the doctrines (and abuses) of Rome in 1517 with his 'religion for the common man'; he was followed in 1530 by Calvin and his 'Protestant' church, while Henry VIII declared himself Head of the English Church in 1534.

The Roman Catholic answer to this 'protesting' activity was the movement known as the 'Counter-Reformation', which resulted in an upsurge of conservative militant faith, reflected in the sacred music of Palestrina (1525–94), Victoria (1548–1611), Lassus (1532–94) and G. Gabrieli (1555–1612), among many.

These composers sought by various means to write 'grave, pious, and distinct' church music, as advocated by the Council of Trent (1545–63), and produced the fine flowering of countless masses and motets. Meanwhile, more adventurous compositions were to be found in the field of secular music, especially the madrigal, where composers sought to extend the scope of emotional expression through experimentation with chromaticism and dissonance.

Although music was believed to speak a universal language (as advocated by the Church, its main patron), it must be stressed that several distinct styles nevertheless emerged during this period. In particular, English composers, from Dunstable onwards, showed an independence of thought which was reflected in the highly individual style of Tallis and Byrd, composers who, in the interests of expression, evolved their own specific treatment of intervals and dissonance.

Before attempting to work in Renaissance style, which may be only slightly familiar to the student, it is essential to have some idea of its 'sound' and character. This is best acquired through singing as many examples as possible; the vocal music represents the style at its best and is readily available.[1] Secular forms, such as madrigals, were intended to be participated in rather than listened to, and, whenever possible, realization should remain the aim, for in performance the spirit of the music comes alive.

The Basic Principles of the Style [2]

The complexities of the Renaissance style may seem formidable, but the principles that evolved by the late 16th century are clear-cut. From the music of Palestrina and the Roman school three important areas become apparent:

(i)   the selection of *intervals* used, in both the melodic (horizontal) and harmonic (vertical) contexts;
(ii) the prevalence of *imitation*;
(iii) the treatment of *dissonance*.

1. INTERVALS

(a) The melody line and horizontal movement

The shapes of the melodic lines, which rise and fall so effectively in this music, are derived from plainsong, the ancient single-lined chant of the Catholic Church, whose influence on the development of Western melody has been profound. The characteristics which governed plainsong also applied to Renaissance melodic lines:

(i)   The melodic movement is dictated by the words; the shape of each phrase is curved, with mainly stepwise movement.
(ii) The compass of the melody rarely exceeds an octave.
(iii) Melodic leaps of a 3rd and perfect 4th are normal, of a 5th (perfect) less common. Leaps of a major 6th, major and minor 7ths, and all augmented and diminished intervals do not occur; a minor 6th occurs as an upward leap only. Any leap is best followed by a step in the opposite direction. No two leaps in the same direction should add up to a major 7th, or exceed an 8ve.
(iv) The rhythm is rarely regular or repetitive since the sequence is not yet a feature of the style. The 'tactus' or 'beat' in the 16th century (a written minim) was always in evidence. It was approximately the same speed as the heart-beat.[3] Modern editions often halve the note values using the crotchet as the tactus.

---

[1] Note the excellent series *Invitation to Madrigals* published by Stainer and Bell.
[2] For a detailed study of this style see Owen Swindale's excellent *Polyphonic Composition* (OUP, 1962).
[3] Nathaniel Tomkins: Preface to *Musica Deo Sacra* (T. Tomkins), 1680.

Sing these examples:

Palestrina: *Missa Papae Marcelli* (1567)

Tactus = 𝅗𝅥

Ky - rie e - lei - son

Palestrina: *Surge illuminare* (1575)

Tactus = 𝅗𝅥

Sur - ge

Tallis: *Lamentations of Jeremiah* (c.1570)

Tactus = 𝅗𝅥

De - la - men - ta - ti - o - ne Ie - re - mi - ae pro - phe - tae

Byrd: *Mass for Five Voices* (c.1595)

Tactus = 𝅗𝅥

Ky - ri - e e - lei - son

(b) The harmonic or vertical progression (two-part writing)

In the past, a study of contrapuntal techniques has included 'species' counterpoint, so named from the treatise by J. Fux called *'Gradus ad Parnassum* (1725), which enumerated the techniques available. This proceeded systematically from very simple, note-against-note counterpoint (1st species) to an elaborate style using imitation, melodic elaboration, and dissonance (5th species); with some modifications, the basic laws thereby established have governed contrapuntal writing for nearly 300 years.

The basic rules may be set out as follows:

(i) The general principle required a consonance between parts or voices on every beat or 'tactus', unless carefully controlled. See p. 11. 'Dissonance'.

(ii) The intervals used were mainly the consonant 3rds and 6ths. Other consonances such as the perfect 5ths and 8ves were confined to weak beats only, because of the thinness of their sound, but the 8ve/unison was common at the beginning and at the cadence.

[4] See 'Musica ficta' , p. 5.

(iii) Parallel or 'consecutive' 5ths or 8ves were not used, since it was believed that they destroyed the independence of the part-writing and created (through repetition of the same interval) a bareness of sonority no longer found desirable in the music. (It had been common practice in music written between 1100 and 1500 to have one melodic line duplicated by another in parallel motion at these intervals, but the practice was forbidden by late Renaissance theorists around 1550, and the 'ban' survived thereafter until the late 19th century.)

(iv) 'Exposed' 5ths and 8ves — occurring when the interval of a (perfect) 5th or 8ve was arrived at in the outside, or 'exposed', parts as the result of a leap in the upper part — were similarly discouraged.

(c) The modes [5]

The church modes or scales (as on the white notes of the piano) on which plainsong was based included the following:

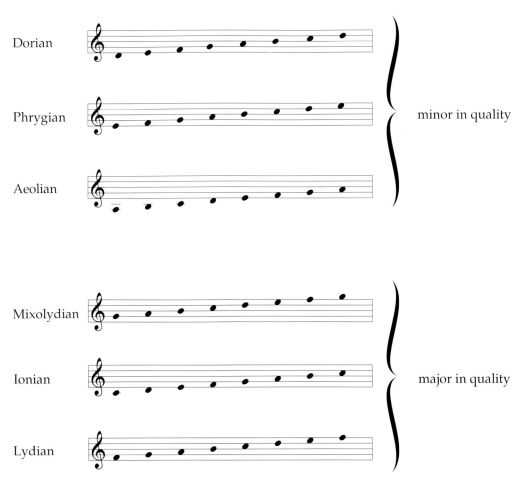

[5] For discussion of this system see Owen Swindale, *Polyphonic Composition*, pp. 50ff.

'*Musica ficta*'. It is believed that in performance accidentals were added, altering B to B♭ in the Lydian mode and giving sharpened leading notes in the modes on D (C♯), G (F♯), and A (G♯), although these were not always written down in the parts. Scholars are still not in agreement on the extent of the application of 'musica ficta'.

The accidentals in question, except for the B♭, were used particularly at cadences, where the semitone pull to the tonic or final was naturally stronger (*a*) and on the final chord as a *tierce de Picardie*, where the minor chord was considered weak (*b*).

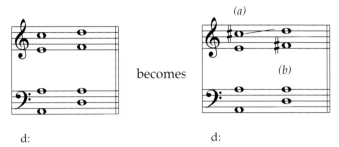

becomes

d: d:

Composers sometimes cadenced on a bare chord containing only the 8ve and the 5th. This tradition was maintained by later composers in contexts where a major chord ending was perhaps inappropriate; examples include the final chord of 'When I am laid in earth' from Purcell's *Dido and Aeneas* and the endings of several minor-key movements in Mozart's *Requiem*.

By the 16th century, the modal system had reached a transitional stage, with the individual qualities of the modes being clouded by the increased use of 'musica ficta', so that two scales only, our major and minor, were in common use in the succeeding tonal era.

Modal key signatures. These are the result of transposition of modes, originally to suit the range of the voice. For example, the Dorian mode transposed into the tenor range, i.e. down a 5th to G, needs a B♭; transposed again into the bass range, i.e. down a further 5th to C, it takes a signature of two flats.

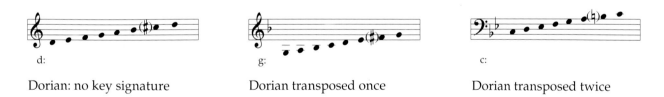

d: g: c:

Dorian: no key signature   Dorian transposed once   Dorian transposed twice

Students will observe that this practice was retained into the Baroque period: see examples of Bach's settings of modal chorales R.49, 110, 174, and 185.[6] Handel uses a key signature of three flats in the F minor chorus 'Surely He hath borne our griefs' in *Messiah* (1742), using accidentals for D♭s.

---

[6] R.= number in A. Riemenschneider, *371 Harmonized Chorales and 69 Chorale Melodies with Figured Bass by J. S. Bach* (London, Schirmer, 1941).

Exercises

Add a second part, creating a note-against-note texture (1st species).

1   *Pange Lingua Gloriosi:* Office hymn

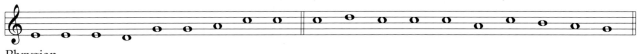

Phrygian

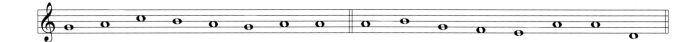

2   *Veni, Creator Spiritus:* Office hymn

Mixolydian

3   Thomas of Celano: 'Dies Irae', in *Requiem* (13th cent.)

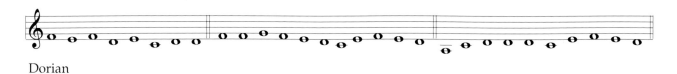

Dorian

(d) Melodic decoration

In 2nd and 3rd species, melodic decoration in the form of *passing, auxiliary,* and *harmony* notes was added to the accompanying part, creating first two, then four notes in counterpoint to each note of the 'cantus firmus' or melody line. 'Passing' notes (p.n.) were so called since they passed up or down (generally down) by step between two consonances a 3rd apart. 'Auxiliary' notes (a.n.) decorated or drew attention to a consonance by movement up or down and back to the same consonance. Both the above decorations were usually dissonant with the melody note, and therefore would *never leap*. 'Harmony' notes (h.n.), however, since they involved a move to another note consonant with the melody notes, might leap:

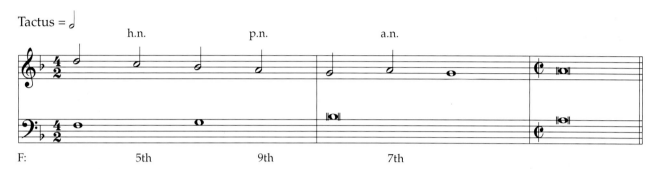

Quavers were used very sparingly. They usually occurred in pairs to decorate a cadence:

Lassus: *Magnum Opus Musicum* (1604)

Exercises

Add a second part using some melodic decoration in the form of passing, auxiliary, and harmony notes (2nd species).

4 Cantus firmus from *Aeterna Christi Munera*, Office hymn.

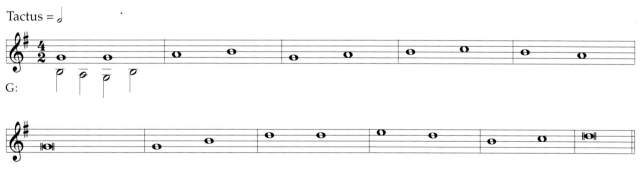

Continue the second part in crotchets (3rd species). Alternate crotchets (marked 'X') should be consonant with the cantus firmus and should not be quitted by an upward leap.

5   Cantus firmus from *Christe Redemptor*, Office hymn

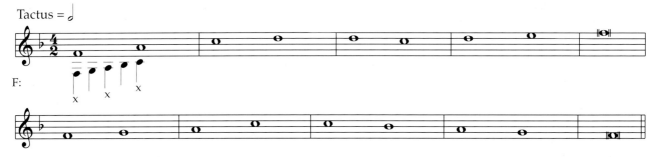

The plainsong canti firmi on p. 6 provide further exercise material.

2. IMITATION

(*a*) Imitation was used in Medieval music and, as the Renaissance progressed, became an integral part of musical texture. Every verbal phrase had its musical counterpart which, when introduced in turn by each voice, became a 'point' of imitation. In the late Renaissance, the new 'points', usually introducing new words, which took over from the earlier ones, emerged out of the preceding part-writing, or counterpointing, resulting in a piece of 'through-imitation'.

(*b*) The imitation usually occurred within the equivalent of two bars' distance; at least the first four or five notes of the point were involved. Opening imitations tended to be strict, i.e. the intervals were copied exactly, tone for tone, semitone for semitone.

Sing this example:

Lassus: *Jesu nostra redemptio* (1567)

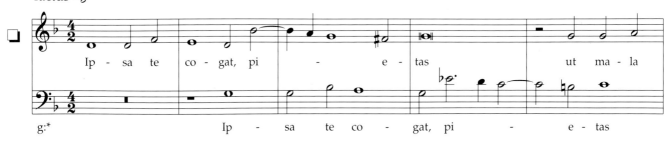

* Modal key signature.

11

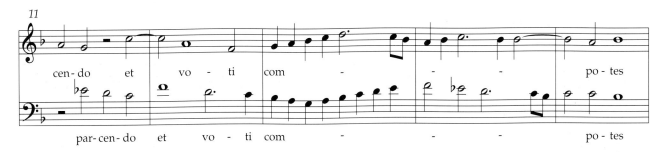

(c) Imitation occurred at the 8ve but was more common at the 5th and 4th. The nature of the subject might decide the interval of imitation; e.g. a subject moving upwards by step was often imitated at the 5th, and one moving downwards imitated at the 4th, but there is no hard and fast rule. The student should experiment with different intervals in the exercises attempted.

(d) The 'tonal answer'— the name given to an altered imitative entry in fugal writing — was established in the late Renaissance. This usually occurs when the subject moves between the tonic and dominant and is imitated ('answered') by a move between dominant and tonic, or vice versa:

Palestrina: Mass, *Regina Coeli* (? 1575)

(e) *Rhythm.* Parts should complement each other rhythmically moving in contrary motion wherever possible. Syncopation is an important trait. Notice the intervals used, both within and between the parts, the complementary part-writing, and the cadence progression in the following example.

Sing this example from Lassus's *Magnum Opus Musicum*, published by his sons in 1604, ten years after his death:

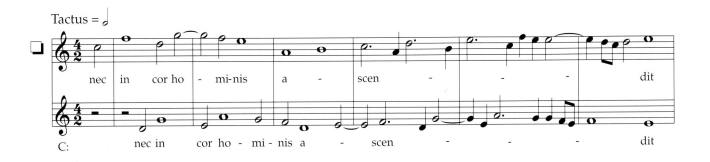

Exercises

Work these passages in two parts, including an imitative entry in each.

6 Monteverdi: *Angelus ad Pastores* (1582)

Tactus = 𝅗𝅥

7 Lassus: Seventh Penitential Psalm (1584)

Tactus = 𝅘𝅥

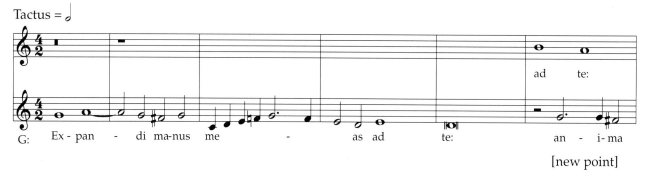

[new point]

8 Lassus: *Magnum Opus Musicum* (1604)

Tactus = 𝅘𝅥

9 Ibid.

Tactus = 𝅗𝅥

* Modal key signature.

10 Palestrina: Mass, *Aeterna Christi Munera* (1590)

3. DISSONANCE

The rise and fall of the melodic line and the unifying principle of through-imitation, together with the role of dissonance with syncopation, combine to realize the sound of late Renaissance music.

(a) Prepared dissonance : the suspension (4th species)

At various stages in Western musical history different intervals have been classified as dissonant: by 1600 these included 4ths, 7ths, and 9ths (2nds) which all required particular treatment, namely downward resolution onto consonances.

The most telling dissonances are those which occur on strong beats: in the Renaissance the only dissonance on an accented beat was a prepared one, i.e. the suspension. Three steps were involved:

(i)   the preparation as a consonance on a weak beat;

(ii) the percussion (or sounding) of the suspension, a dissonance, on a strong beat;

(iii) the resolution, moving down by step to a consonance, on a beat weaker than the suspension itself:

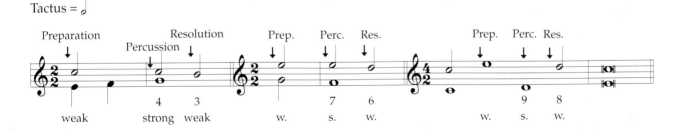

The suspension may be seen as a decoration of the harmony and will always involve some element of syncopation, which adds to the tension created by the dissonance and imparts a rhythmic vitality peculiar to the music of the period. The powerful effect of dissonance as a means of creating tension was fully appreciated by the madrigalists, for example, who realized the expressive possibilities of the idiom:

T. Morley: *Fire! fire!* (1595)

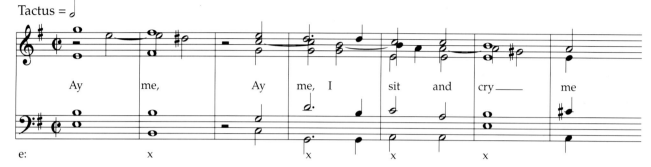

Suspensions often occur in 'chains' (see also Exercises 12 and 13):

Bass suspensions are most effective when the resolution forms a 3rd.

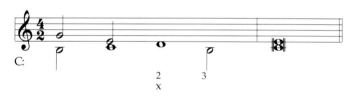

A cadence should always be decorated with a suspension. Morley emphasizes this in his *A Plaine and Easie Introduction to Practicall Musick* (1597), citing the 7–6 suspension as a common example: 'There is no coming to a close without a discord, and that most commonly a seventh bound in with your sixth as your plainsong descendeth.'

Lassus: *Magnum Opus Musicum* (1604)

Exercise

11   Copy down examples of cadences from the pieces you have studied.

Decorations of the suspension formula itself include:

(i)   The half-beat anticipation note, anticipating either the note of preparation (*a*),
      or the note of resolution (*b*), or both, in a 'chain'.

Byrd: *Mass for Four Voices* (c.1592)

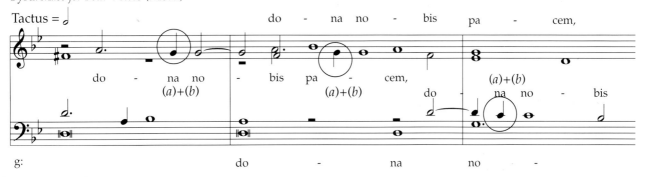

(ii) The use of quavers, which only ever move by step, to ornament the melody
      line. These usually occur in pairs, taking the place of an unaccented crotchet
      or quaver after a dotted minim or dotted crotchet (see the Lassus example
      below).

Lassus: *Expectatio justorum* (1577)

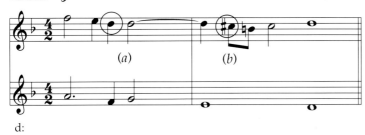

(iii) The changing of the bass note under the note of resolution. This may imply
      a change of inversion, or even of 'harmony' when more than two parts are
      involved:

Byrd: *Ave verum corpus* (1605)

Exercises

Identify and figure the suspensions in the following extracts.

12 Morley: *I should for grief* (1595)

13 Lassus: *Expectatio justorum* (1577)

A chord characteristic of the period can occur when a prepared dissonance sounds between the upper parts, i.e. when the bass is not involved in the dissonance (x):

Palestrina: Mass, *Aeterna Christi Munera* (1590)

This example also shows a rare use of the diminished triad in root position (]), and forms the basis of a cadence formula found frequently in Bach's chorales, viz. IV⁷b–V⁷b–I:

Bach: R. 50

Double suspensions may occur, the most common being in 3rds and 6ths, as in the example below. Note also the characteristic word-painting in this madrigal excerpt:

Tomkins: *Weep no more* (1622)
Tactus = ♩

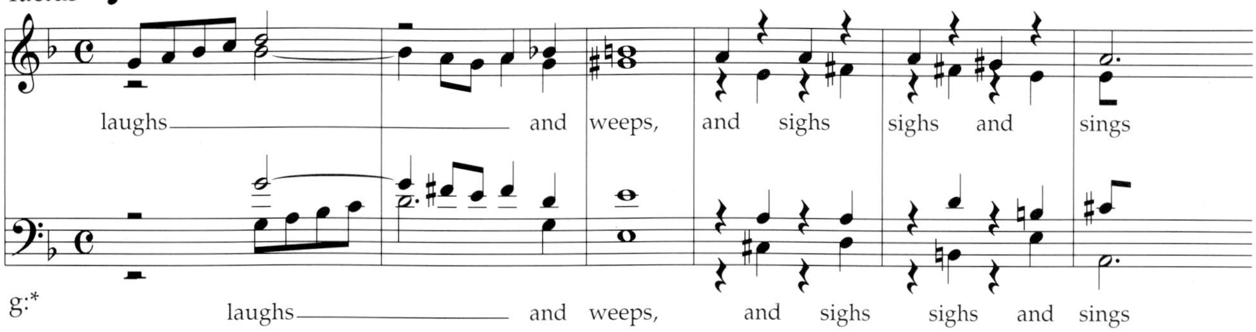

Exercises

14 ❑ Sing or play through the examples in this section, noting the characteristic cadence formulae.

Complete the following extracts using imitative entries and suspensions as indicated.

15 Palestrina: *Exultate Deo* (1584)
Tactus = 𝅗𝅥

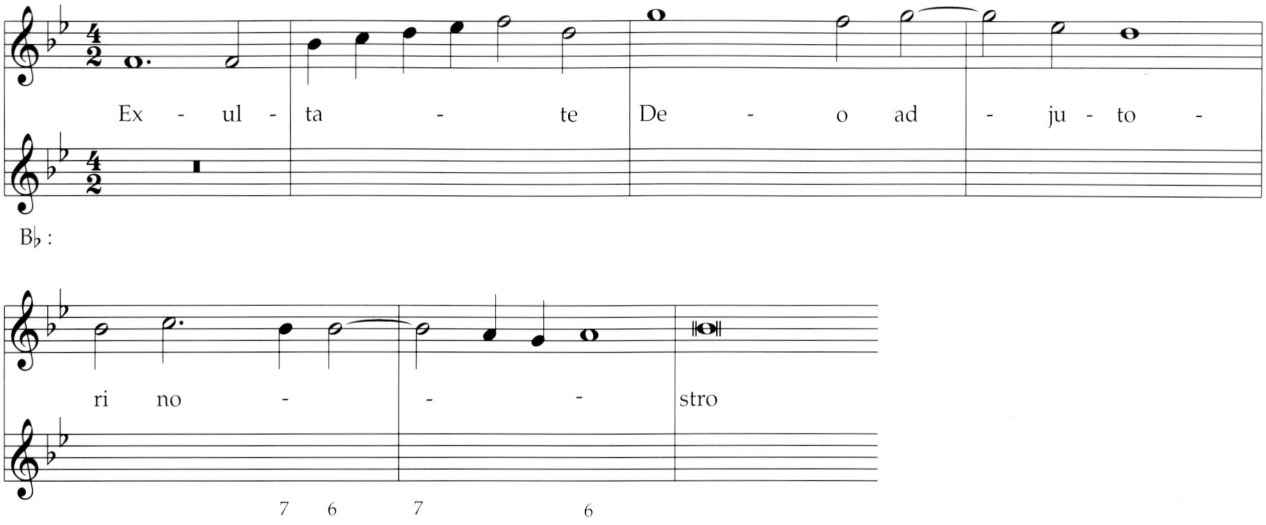

16 Byrd: *Mass for Five Voices* (*c.*1595)

Tactus = 𝅗𝅥

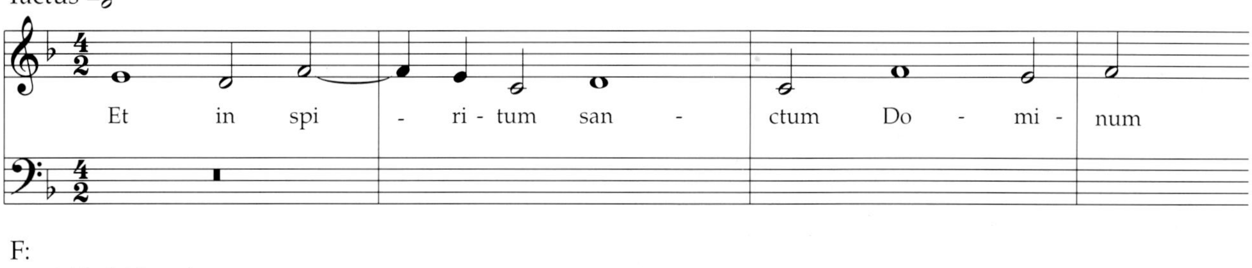

* Modal key signature.

17   Redford: *Rejoice in the Lord* (from a keyboard piece in the Mulliner Book (*c*.1550–75))
Tactus = 𝅗𝅥

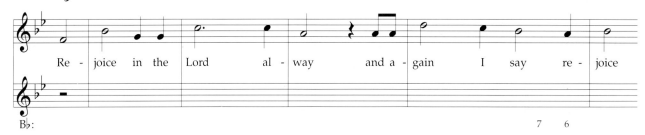

18   Palestrina: Mass, *Aeterna Christi Munera* (1590)
Tactus = 𝅗𝅥

19   Ibid
Tactus = 𝅗𝅥

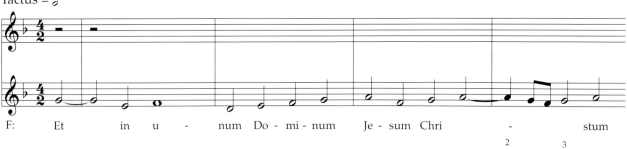

Further exercises in two to four vocal parts are included at the end of this chapter.

(b) Unprepared dissonance

Unprepared dissonance was restricted to the weaker beats of the bar in Renaissance music, a characteristic frequently retained in later music. Examples include:

 (i)   the accented passing note;
 (ii) the 'nota cambiata';
 (iii) the anticipation note;
 (iv) the 'consonant 4th'.

 (i)   *Accented passing note.* This occurs moving by step, usually as part of a des-
       cending line on the weaker beats; e.g. in 4/2 time on the second and fourth
       minim. It generally appears as a crotchet; quavers figure only rarely:

Hilton: *Lord for thy tender mercies sake* (? 1594)

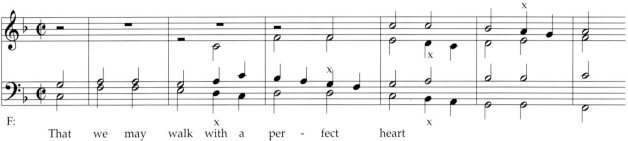

That   we   may   walk   with   a   per - fect   heart

Exercises

Identify the accented passing notes in the following examples.

20 Lassus: *Magnum Opus Musicum* (1604)

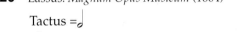

G:

21 Ibid.

B♭:

Minim accented passing notes are practically absent from two-part writing. Long passing notes creating dissonance do occur, often passing over stationary notes in the texture (*a* and *b*). Passages of 'organum' (progressions of first-inversion chords) sometimes move in this way to great effect (*c*).

(*a*) Palestrina: *Aeterna Christi Munera* (1590)

F:

(*b*) Tomkins: *When David heard* (1622)

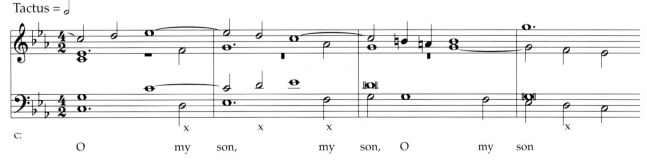

c:

O   my   son,   my   son,   O   my   son

(c) Tallis: *Lamentations of Jeremiah* (? 1570)

Tactus =

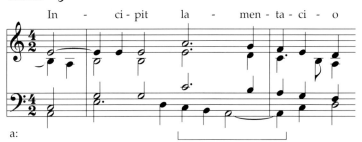

(ii) '*Nota cambiata*'. This characteristic figure, meaning 'changed' note, is the only case (in this style) of a dissonance quitted by a leap. It is frequently used in figurations and decorative patterns, where its shape is always the same (and tends to involve what would later be understood as the 7th of the dominant or a secondary chord). The 'nota cambiata' is often found in conjunction with a suspension:

Morley: *Out of the Deep* (?1593)

Tactus =

Exercise

Identify the cambiata figure in the following passage:

22 Tomkins: *When David heard* (1622)

Tactus =

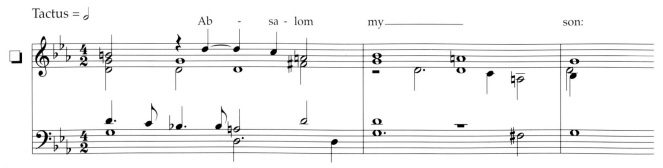

(iii) *Anticipation note*. This may create a passing dissonance. It is effective at the cadence, particularly where the tonic is sounded against the leading note.

Gibbons: *The Silver Swan* (1612)
Tactus = 𝅗𝅥

F:

Fifty years later, Purcell adopted the same idiom, to great effect.

Purcell: *Rejoice in the Lord* (c.1683)
(Moderato)

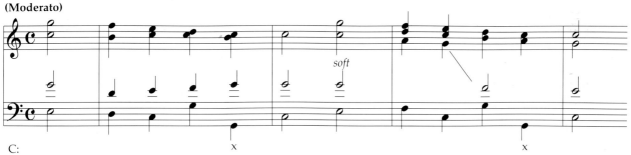

C:

(iv) *'Consonant 4th'*. The overwhelming desire to include dissonance at the cadence, even when preparation was impossible, resulted in the formula known as the 'consonant 4th'. This consists of an unprepared 4th approached by step over a stationary bass. A third voice is necessary, to create on the 3rd beat of the bar (or half-bar) a further dissonance (7th or 2nd) with the voice singing the 4th. Thereafter the 4th resolves, like a normal suspension, at the end of the bar. (It may be helpful to think of the consonant 4th as another, but rather more extended version of the anticipation note, involving the 'final' or tonic.) Note that in the first example below, the tactus is treated as a crotchet beat during the formula.

Byrd: *Mass for Four Voices* (c.1592)
Tactus = 𝅗𝅥

g:

Palestrina: Mass, *Aeterna Christi Munera* (1590)
Tactus = 𝅗𝅥

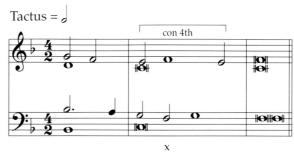

F:

Two other common types of dissonance should be mentioned at this point, the augmented triad and false relations.

The augmented triad. The movement of parts or voices, analysed vertically, sometimes creates an unusual chord, which is then utilized in a specific way. Such a chord is iiib (minor key), whose augmented interval is usually employed to heighten the meaning of the text and belongs, therefore, particularly to the language of the madrigalists.

Exercises

Identify the chord in the examples below.

23 Tomkins: *Then David mourned* (? 1620)

24 Gibbons: *The Silver Swan* (1612)

'Cross' or false relations. This dissonance (part of the tonal ambiguity already mentioned, under *'Musica ficta'* above) usually involved the sounding, either simultaneously or in close proximity, of the sharpened and flattened leading notes, one rising, the other falling—altered to avoid augmented intervals occurring horizontally. It was particularly common in 16th-century England in the music of Tallis and Byrd, where its use as a cadential formula earned it the title of the 'English cadence'; the dissonance was nevertheless frequently included in works of continental composers for its obvious expressive effect, and hence, like the augmented triad, often figures in Renaissance madrigals. Purcell inherited this so-called 'roughness' of style, and examples are to be found in the music of Lully and the French Baroque; in fact cross relations are not uncommon even in later 18th-century music (as the Mozart example below demonstrates). As was often the case, the dissonance, which arose out of the combination of melodic lines, was then exploited for its ability to heighten a text, and was ultimately adopted as part of a composer's musical language simply because it was relished for its own sake.

* Modal key signature.

Tallis: *Lamentations of Jeremiah* (? 1570)

Tactus =

c:

Byrd: *Ave verum corpus* (1605)

Tactus =

a:

Purcell: *Remember not, Lord, our offences* (c. 1680)

(Moderato)

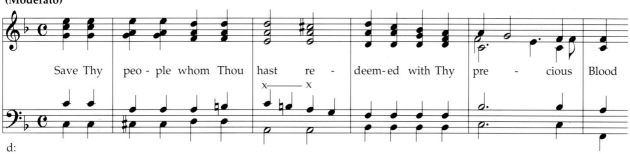

d:

Mozart: *The Magic Flute* (1791)

Andante

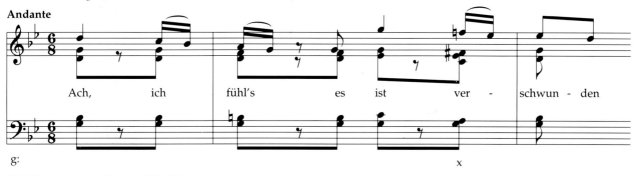

g:

('O, I know it, love has vanished')

Exercise

25 Comment on the effectiveness of the word-setting in the following passage from Dowland's 'In Darkness let me Dwell' (1620), for solo voice with lute accompaniment, indicating the following:

(a) cross relations,
(b) augmented triads,
(c) suspensions,
(d) long passing notes,
(e) 'modulations',
(f) anticipation notes.

Other Features of the Style

1. CHROMATIC WRITING

The use of chromaticism as a potent means of expression was firmly established by Renaissance composers in their vocal compositions, and indeed continued throughout the tonal era. It became associated with the emotions of grief and despair and with the depiction of the weird and fantastical, particularly when notes from the *descending* scale were used.

Towards the end of the 16th century, experiments were made in the tuning of keyboard instruments which led to the acceptance of equal temperament. N. Vicentino, possibly a pupil of Willaert, invented the arcicembalo, a keyboard instrument with *six* manuals, whose chromatic qualities were supposed to have influenced Gesualdo, the most 'extreme' of the Italian madrigalists:

Gesualdo: *Dolcissima mia vita* (1611)

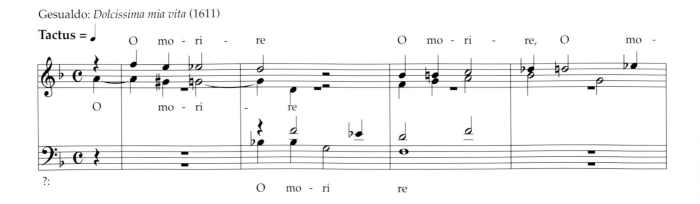

(O, to die!)

Weelkes: *Thule, the period of cosmography* (1600)

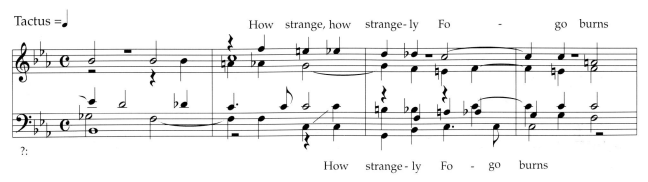

2. THE HARMONIC 'INSTINCT'

Although 1600–1900 is often quoted as the period of tonal music, it is evident that composers before this date, as far back as Pérotin (d. *c.*1225) and Machaut (d. 1377), conceived much of their music harmonically, with a key or tonal centre in evidence, particularly at the cadence. Equally, many 20th-century composers, such as Benjamin Britten, have retained the tonal system as an effective means of expression.

In the opening of his *Stabat Mater*, Palestrina was patently thinking in terms of an effective *harmonic* progression, while one of the 'moments' in Tallis's forty-part motet, *Spem in alium*, is a purely harmonic one—the drop from C major to A major on the words 'Respice humilitatem nostram' (be mindful of our lowliness):

Tallis: *Spem in alium* (?1573)

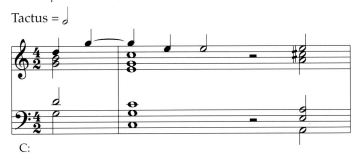

Palestrina: *Stabat Mater* (?1570)

Tactus = ♩

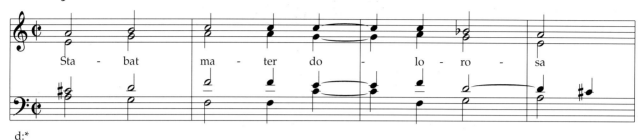

d:*

(The weeping mother stood by the cross)

A study of modal harmony requires a volume to itself, but two common features of the harmonic idiom along with the chords already mentioned should be noted:

(*a*) The prevalence of the chord on the flattened leading note (which also survived into the 18th century):

Palestrina: *Exultate Deo* (1584)

Tactus = ♩

B♭ :

Handel stepped back into Purcell's shoes in this wonderful phrase from the *Utrecht Te Deum* (1713):

Andante

D: Heav'n and earth are full of the ma - jes - ty of Thy Glo - ry

(*b*) The frequency of such progressions as ii–I, V–IV, and iii–I or I–iii:

Palestrina: Mass, *Aeterna Christi Munera* (1590)

Tactus = ♩

C: V IV

F: vi I   iii

* Dorian mode—no key signature.

3. NOTE DOUBLING

When writing for three or more parts, composers generally avoided doubling notes of motion such as leading notes, (dominant) 7ths, dissonances, and chromatically altered notes because:

(*a*) these notes were already prominent and doubling them upset the balance of the chord;

(*b*) notes of motion, as their name suggests, need to move either up (leading notes), or down (7ths and most dissonances such as suspensions): if they are doubled, and correctly resolved, consecutive movement will result.

The major 3rd (when not appearing as a leading note) was frequently doubled, but usually quitted in contrary motion. (It is usually doubled in chord VI in a minor key, when the progression moves V–VI.)

Exercises

Work these passages in four parts (S.A.T.B.), labelling the chords used (with roman numerals). Remember to include suspensions at cadences where possible.

26 John Farmer: *Fair Phyllis* (1599)

27 J. Bennet: *All creatures now* (1601)

28 T. Ford: *Since first I saw your face* (1607)

Tactus =

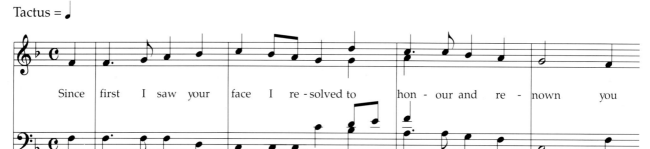

Since first I saw your face I re-solved to hon - our and re - nown you

F:

29 J. Dowland: *Fine knacks for ladies* (1600)

Tactus =

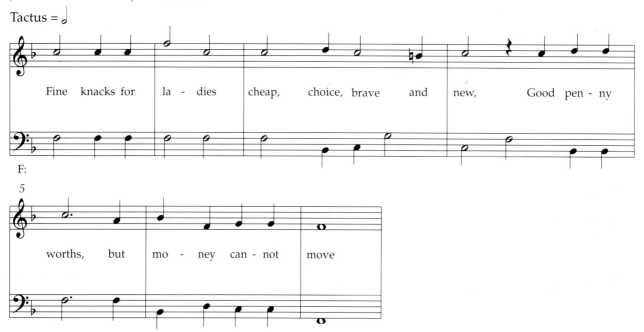

Fine knacks for la - dies cheap, choice, brave and new, Good pen - ny

F:

5

worths, but mo - ney can - not move

The crotchet is constant.

Complete in five parts.

30 Tallis: *Lamentations of Jeremiah* (? 1570)

Tactus =

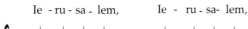

Ie - ru - sa - lem, Ie - ru - sa - lem, -

Ie - ru - sa - lem, Ie - ru - sa - lem, con - ver - te - re ad Do - mi - num De - um tu - um

F/d:

Jerusalem, return again to the Lord thy God.

Complete in two parts.

31 Lassus: Fantasia No. 1 (1577)

Tactus = 𝅗𝅥

d:

32 Lassus: Fantasia No. 3 (1577)

Tactus = 𝅗𝅥

G:

33   Lassus: Fantasia No. 5 (1577)

34   Morley: *Canzonets for Two Voices* (1595)

* Modal key signature.

35 Ibid.

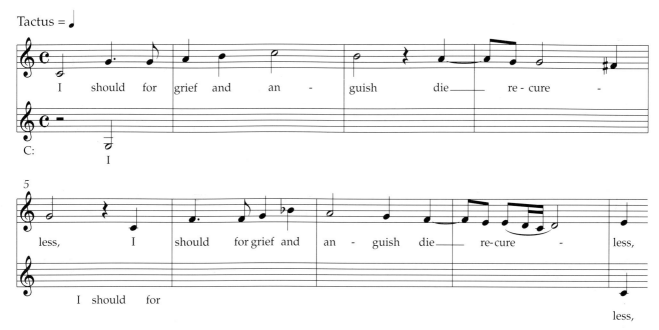

36 Ibid.

37   Byrd: *Mass for Four Voices* (c.1592)

Complete for three voices.

38   Palestrina: Mass, *Aeterna Christi Munera* (1590)

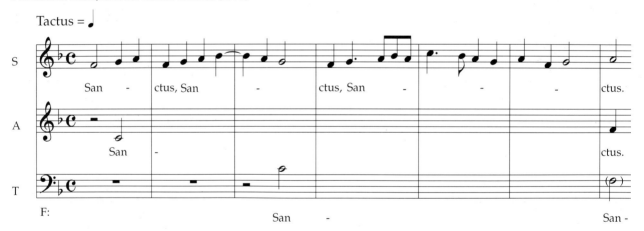

39   Ibid.

40   Weelkes: *Those sweet delightful lilies* (1597)

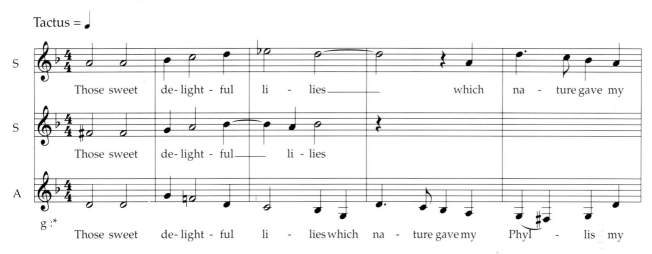

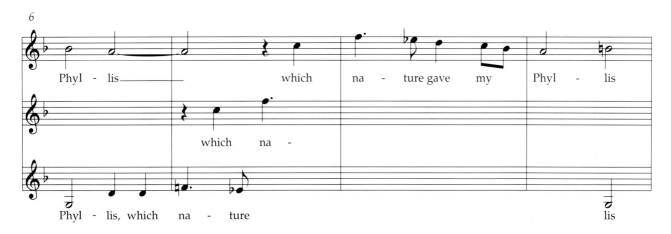

* Modal key signature.

41   Morley: *Though Philomena lost her love* (1593)

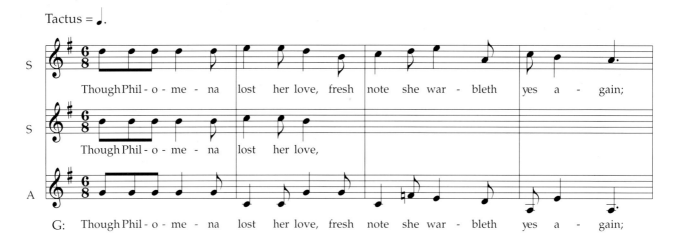

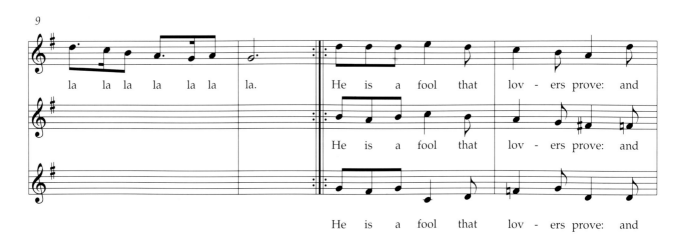

13

leaves to sing, to live in pain. Fa la la la la la la la la la la la la la la la la

Fa la la la la la la la

Fa la la la la la la la

17

la la la la la la Fa la la la la la la la. la.

Fa la la la la la la la la.

42   J. Ward: *Fly not so fast* (1613)

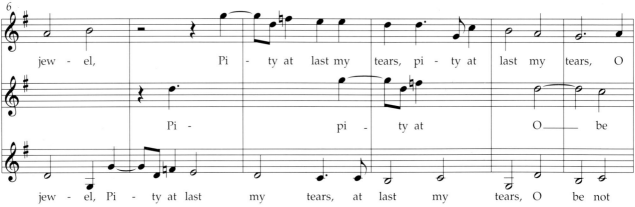

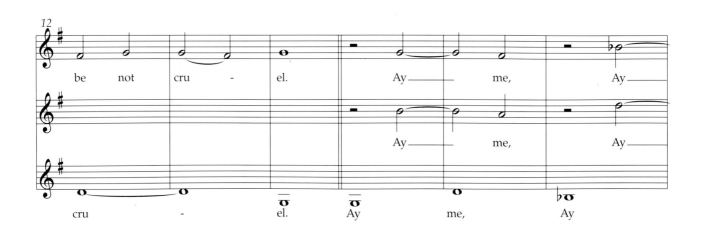

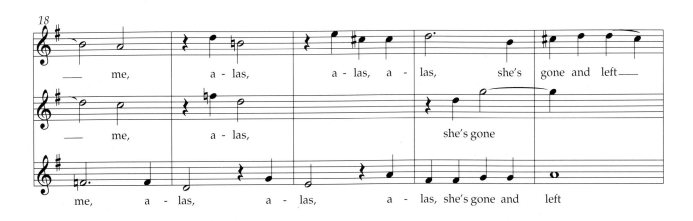

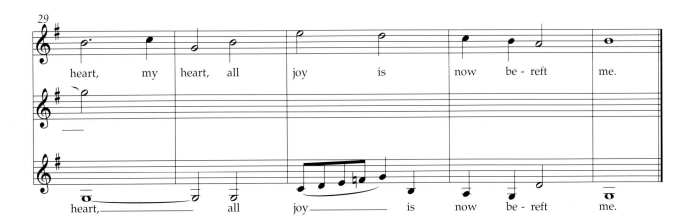

43 T. Tomkins: *Love, cease tormenting* (1622)

Complete for S.A.T.B.

44 T. Bateson: *Phyllis, farewell* (1604)

* Modal key signature.

2. The Baroque Period
(c.1600–1750)

From the 1570s Renaissance and early Baroque styles coexisted, with the latter calling for more passionate and exuberant treatment. The difference between the two may be summed up in two remarkable pieces of sculpture: *La Pietà* of Michelangelo, a masterpiece of the Renaissance which is none the less detached and impassive; and *The Ecstasy of St Teresa* of Bellini, a Baroque work which seeks to involve the onlooker by its powerful sense of movement and passion. 'Baroque' is a term used to describe the lavish style of art and architecture in the 17th and early 18th centuries; adopted by music historians, it covers the same extensive period and speaks the same eloquent language, rich in colour and spectacle, seeking to captivate and involve the listener, whether he be an ardent Jesuit, Lutheran, or opera-lover .

This new concept of involving the listener as well as the participant was one of the chief aims of the Camerata, the group of early opera writers based in Florence, and was expressed in Caccini's *Le Nuove Musiche* (1602). Since 1500, composers, and madrigal composers especially, had sought to underline aspects of the text by musical means. After 1600 the theory of the 'affections' crystallized, categorizing the emotions to be expressed in music into recognized states of mind, such as anger, hate, jealousy, joy, or despair. In most compositions of this period an 'affection' governed a whole movement. The text of Purcell's *Ode on St Cecilia's Day* (1692), written by Nicholas Brady, claims that the role of music, the 'mighty art', is 'to court the ear, or strike the heart, at once the passions to express and move. We hear and straight we grieve or hate, rejoice or love.'

The Baroque was a period also characterized by the birth and development of many vocal and instrumental forms, including opera, oratorio, cantata, concerto, and suite. The upsurge in instrumental writing stemmed from the development of instruments (especially the violin family), around which the group gradually recognizable as the orchestra formed, and the consequent expansion of available instrumental skills. Both early Baroque and early Classical compositions were reactions against the complex music they succeeded—the early Baroque against late Renaissance polyphony, and the early Classical against the intricacies of late Baroque counterpoint. Both initially reverted to a simple style, melody-dominated and supported by a bass-line.

The Musical Language of the Baroque: Music Based on Triads

Around 1600 a shift from the older 'horizontal' polyphonic style to vertical or harmonic musical thinking involved the recognition and use of triads as the basis of musical composition. This led to further exciting experiments with chords for expressive purposes, and to the establishment of a diatonic tonality in which keys and key relationships were to dominate musical composition for some 250 years. Dissonance too, now frequently unprepared, was used to enhance expression. Monteverdi's aria *Lasciate mi morire* (1608) illustrates this new freedom of harmonic thought.

Monteverdi: *Arianna* (1608)

d:
(Leave me to die)

1. THE CONTINUO AND FIGURED BASS

The most obvious manifestation of harmonic dominance was the general acceptance of the 'basso continuo' throughout the period in all except solo instrumental music. Two players provided the continuo, which usually included a bass instrument (such as a viola da gamba) and a keyboard. The player of the latter 'realised' the 'figured' bass, filling in the harmonies implied by the figures. (The realization in modern editions is usually supplied by the editor.)
Note:

- (a) In the early Baroque period, basses were left largely unfigured; sometimes first inversions were figured with a 6.
- (b) The figured bass realization did not double the melodic line, leaving the soloist free to decorate or improvize as he wished; nor did it double notes of motion (at pitch) such as leading notes and dissonances.

2. INTERPRETATION OF FIGURED BASS

- (a) The figures (with the highest number on top) represent the intervals when counted from the bass note. The notes of the triad may be disposed between the parts in any order.
- (b) A root-position chord is usually signified by an unfigured bass, but $\frac{5}{3}$ may follow $\frac{6}{4}$ to indicate the resolution of this 'unstable' inversion.
- (c) The figuring for $\frac{6}{3}$, the first inversion of the triad, is usually reduced to 6, but $\frac{6}{4}$, denoting the second inversion, retains both numerals.
- (d) An accidental on its own affects the note a 3rd above the bass note.
- (e) An accidental next to a number affects that specific interval, e.g. ♮6 indicates that the 6th should be raised after a flat, or lowered after a sharp. Similarly, a diagonal stroke through a figure, e.g. 6̸ indicates sharpening.

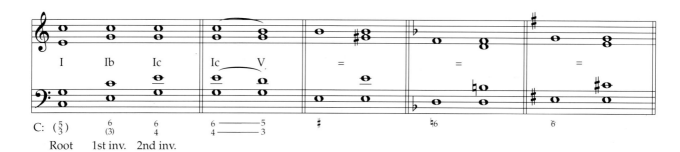

I   Ib   Ic   Ic   V

C: $\binom{5}{3}$ $\begin{smallmatrix}6\\(3)\end{smallmatrix}$ $\begin{smallmatrix}6\\4\end{smallmatrix}$ $\begin{smallmatrix}6\\4\end{smallmatrix}$——5/3   ♯   ♮6   6̄

Root   1st inv.   2nd inv.

(*f*) Suspension figurings are 9–(8), 7–6, and 4–(3); care must be taken to prepare the dissonance in the part in which it is to occur.

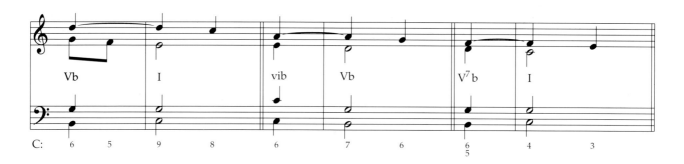

Vb   I   vib   Vb   V⁷b   I

C: 6   5   9   8   6   7   6 $\begin{smallmatrix}6\\5\end{smallmatrix}$ 4   3

Exercises

Label the chords with roman numerals. Add one inner part to realize the harmony. Suspensions should be prepared.

45   Monteverdi: *Il ballo delle Ingrate* (1608)

(Lento)

A - er   se - re - no e   pu - ro!

B♭:   4   3

46   Schütz: *The Christmas Story* (1664)

(Moderato)

Now let us praise   Him and with   all the an - gels,   Sing in the high - est!

F: 6   ♭   ♯

47   Purcell: *Dido and Aeneas* (1689)

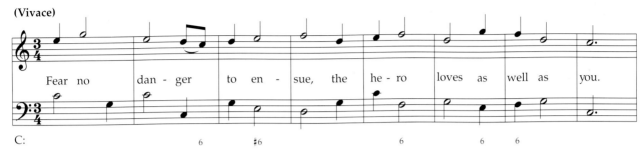

48   Purcell: *The Fairy Queen* (1692)

3. THE CHORD OF THE DOMINANT 7th

The dominant chord holds a special place in the key; the formula V^7–I is the fundamental harmonic progression in music of the tonal era (see p. 11). The satisfaction the ear obtains from the progression derives from the positions of the roots. The 5th of the scale is the strongest note in the harmonic series apart from the 8ve, with a natural 'pull' towards its fundamental, hence the strength of V–I. The other notes of motion in the dominant 7th chord include the leading note, with its semitone 'pull' up to the tonic, and the minor 7th, a dissonance above the root, which needs to be resolved downwards:

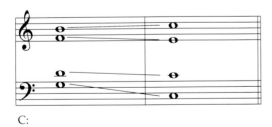

The dominant 7th's chief function is to reinforce the sense of the key to which it belongs; it is unique in that its diatonic 'spelling' can belong to and describe one key only.

In the Renaissance the 7th, as a dissonance, was required to be prepared. Monteverdi and the early opera writers, in seeking greater means of musical expression, shook off this convention, and the dominant 7th emerged as an independent chord with its own special sound.

Monteverdi: *Orfeo* Act V (1607)

(alas, sorrow, alas, plaint)

However, even Bach, a hundred years later, treated V⁷ in root position as a rather special chord. Often he prepared the 7th or added it as a passing note (see Chapter 3). It was only later, in the 19th century, that frequent use of the dominant 7th led to its devaluation.

Inversions, figurings, and resolutions

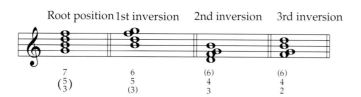

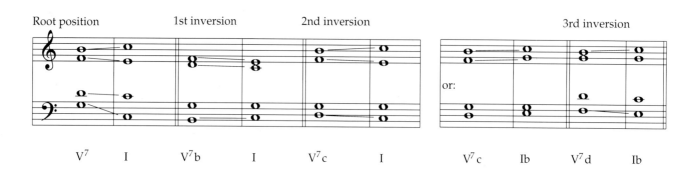

All these inversions are used freely. Note that in the progression V⁷c–Ib the 7th may rise. V⁷d, a favourite chord of Handel, normally resolves on to the first inversion of the tonic chord. Like chord viib, the inversions of V⁷ are particularly useful when a composer wishes to avoid the sense of 'close' created by V⁷ in root position. Since the dominant 7th chord defines key so positively, it is most important in achieving convincing modulation.

Exercises

Identify the keys, together with their dominant 7th chords and their inversions, in this impressive passage. Sing it through.

49   Purcell: *Remember not, Lord, our offences* (?1680)

Fill in alto and tenor parts from the figures (the original is in five parts). Check for possible consecutives.

50   Monteverdi: Psalm, *Beatus vir* (1640)

(Blessed is the man that feareth the Lord)

Realize this figured bass for four string parts, completing a strong melody line first. Phrase the extract whilst singing it through, and note the keys and harmonic progressions, such as sequences, used. Finally identify any chords requiring special treatment.

51 Schütz: Symphonia from *The Seven Last Words* (1645)

(Moderato)

4. SOME CHARACTERISTICS OF BAROQUE MELODY

In the Renaissance, imitation between voices was used mainly as a device to draw attention to the various phrases of text. However, Baroque composers quickly realized the potential of the repeated pattern (varied in pitch) as a means of extending a single musical line, and the sequence — which could be melodic, and now also harmonic (see 'Functional Harmony' below) — became a favourite feature. Like the earlier 'point', it could be either an exact (real) sequence, or one in which the intervals were slightly altered to allow for harmonic moves between major and minor triads or repetition stepwise on various degrees of the scale (tonal sequence):

Bach: Prelude No. 4, '48', Book 1 (1722)

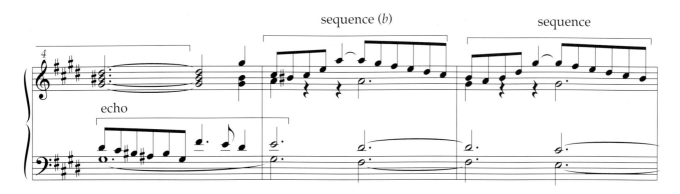

Besides sequences, Baroque melodic lines contain many repeated phrases and 'echoes', and elaborate passages of melodic decoration and figuration. Frequently, composers did not differentiate between the lines they wrote for voices and those given to instruments, thus making much of the music of this period very difficult to sing. In Bach's Cantata No. 51, *Jauchzet Gott* (c.1730), for example, the voice almost 'competes' with the trumpet!

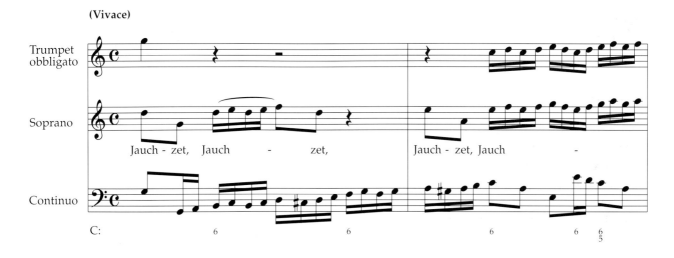

(Praise God)

A few composers did write effective melodies for a particular medium, however; for example, Corelli wrote music for the violin which demonstrated both its lyrical and dynamic qualities, while Purcell and Handel wrote for the voice with supreme skill:

Corelli: Violin Sonata Op. 5 No. 8 (1700)

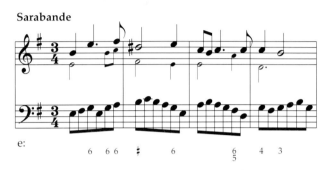

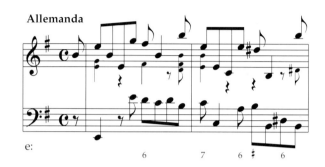

Purcell's melodic genius is revealed in songs and choruses from his dramatic music. His particular gift was to capture the essence of the words in a highly individual way, whether he was setting a love-song, a lament, or an evocation of mood, as in the following extract from 'Sleep' from *The Fairy Queen* (1692). Notice the effect of the rests, and of the hypnotic repetition of words:

Handel, also a man of the theatre, wrote to please popular taste, seeking to move and involve his audiences. In this respect his ability to write a good 'tune' was vital to his success and his visit in 1706–10 to Italy — a country obsessed with singing and singers — had a radical impact on his style. With German his native language, his English word-setting cannot compare with Purcell's, but his melodic gift remains one of his greatest attributes.

Exercise

52   Find examples of melodies by Baroque composers; in what way are they characteristic of this period?

Functional Harmony

Early on in the Baroque period, i.e. from approximately 1620, some important principles were formulated, which then came to dominate harmonic thought and practice. The following points are the main ones which need concern the student.

1. CHORD PROGRESSIONS

The most important principle was the establishment of tonality, achieved through the gradual replacing of the modes with the diatonic system of major and minor scales. The chords in each key in three groups (tonic; dominant: 5th higher; and subdominant: 5th lower) now had specific functions to the tonal centre to which they belonged, and also to each other.

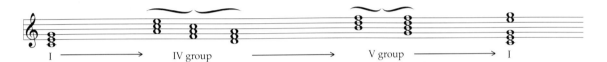

(a) Strong progressions

   (i) *The progression of 5ths.* This progression, a 'sequence' (repeated pattern) of roots with falling 5ths or rising 4ths, is probably the strongest and most natural progression, deriving as it does from the properties of the harmonic series itself; much tonal music is based on it:

I–IV–vii–iii–vi–ii–V–I

The most common version of the progression, its origins lying in the Renaissance, is the cadence formula which uses the end-part of the sequence, viz.: vi or I–iib–V–I. The satisfying nature of the falling 5ths progressions, combined with the pull of the semitone movement — often enhanced by some decorative addition such as a suspension — assured this formula its constant use throughout the tonal era.

Exercises

These early English hymns provide many examples of characteristic cadence progressions; note the suspensions at X. Complete the harmonizations for S.A.T.B. Label the chords.

53 Este's Psalter (1592)

54 Damon's Psalter (1579)

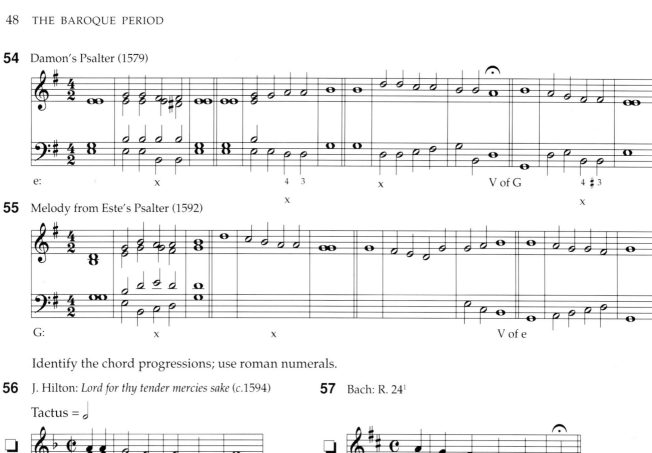

55 Melody from Este's Psalter (1592)

Identify the chord progressions; use roman numerals.

56 J. Hilton: *Lord for thy tender mercies sake* (c.1594)

Tactus = 𝅗𝅥

F:

57 Bach: R. 24[1]

G: D:

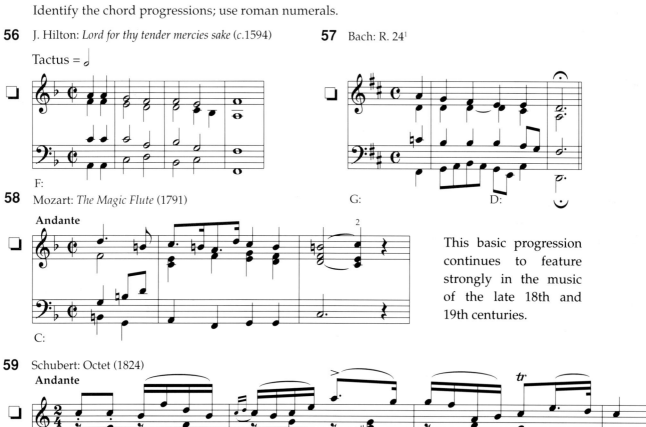

58 Mozart: *The Magic Flute* (1791)

Andante

C:

This basic progression continues to feature strongly in the music of the late 18th and 19th centuries.

59 Schubert: Octet (1824)

Andante

C:

[1] Chorale number in Riemenschneider: see p. 5.
[2] Retardation: see p. 159.

The addition of the 7th, initially to either the dominant or supertonic chord or both, strengthened the progression still further through the pull of the semitones. This could also be achieved through the chromatic alteration of notes in the progressions; e.g. the alteration of the 3rd in ii⁷ makes it the dominant 7th of the dominant.

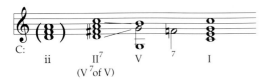

Exercises

Label the cadence chords, noting the 7ths.

60 Handel: *Messiah* (1742)

61 Purcell: *The Fairy Queen* (1692)

62 Bach: R. 242

7ths often occur in sequences in the progression of 5ths. It was usual to prepare the 7th:

Bach: R. 26

Exercises

Label the chord progressions in this passage.

63   Corelli: Violin Sonata Op. 5 No. 11 (1700)

Here is the same progression strengthened by 7ths: label the chords.

64   Ibid.

Label the chords in the following extract.

65   Bach: Prelude No. 16, '48', Book 1 (1722)

Add a right-hand keyboard continuo part, examining the chord progressions.

66 Corelli: Violin Sonata Op. 5 No. 3 (1700)

Complete for S.A.T.B. Label the chords.

67 Purcell: *Ode for St Cecilia's Day* (1692)

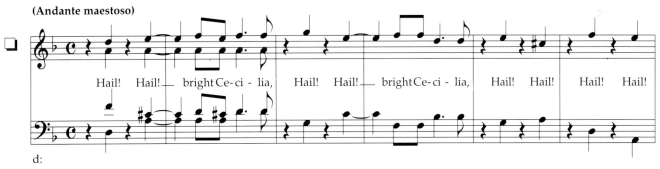

Sing this passage and fill in the harmony for S.A.T.B.

68 Bach: *St John Passion* (1724)

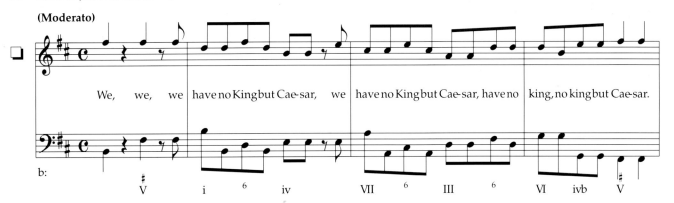

Continue this chain of sequences by Vivaldi.

69   Violin Concerto Op. 3 No. 6 (1712)

e:

(ii) *Scale movements in the bass.* The use of ascending and descending scales in the bass dates back to early part-music. Their strength lies in the sense of direction they give to the music, either towards the dominant or to the tonic, often helped by the upper part moving in contrary motion. Ascending scales usually move between tonic and dominant chords; examples (*a*) and (*b*) below:

(*a*) Bach: R. 39

e: b:

(*b*) Bach: R. 163

g:

Descending scale movements produce particularly strong and satisfying progressions; they generally move from the tonic (*c*) and often include chords associated with the progression of 5ths (*d*).

---

[3] This resolution of the leading note was not uncommon even though it involved the interval of the diminished 4th in the minor key.

(c) Handel: Concerto Grosso Op. 6 No. 10 (1739)

Lento

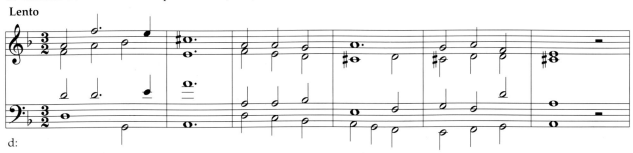

d:

(d) Bach: R. 101

B♭:

(iii) *The ground bass.* The descending scale, particularly, was often used as a 'ground' (a repeating bass on which variations were built) because of the satisfying harmonic progressions that were possible, e.g. i–vb (flattened 7th)–ivb–V:

Purcell: *King Arthur* (1691)

(Moderato)

g: I   Vb   ivb   V

Chromatic movement was included where the 'affect' of the music demanded an emotional response of grief or anguish from the listener. There are many versions of this formula: see also the 'Crucifixus' from the Mass in B minor by Bach.

Purcell: Lament from *Dido and Aeneas* (1689)

(Slow)

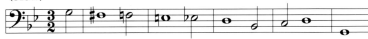

g:

When I am laid in earth

(b) 'Neutral' progressions

Progressions involving *roots rising a 3rd*, e.g. I–iii (i–III), are not common in this style and need care. iii (III) sometimes sounds like an inversion of $I^7(i^7)$ in passing between

I (i) and IV (iv) (see example (*a*) below). iiib may be used as a substitute for the dominant chord, as it contains the leading note over a dominant bass (*b*).

(*a*) Bach: R. 211

(*b*) Purcell: *The Fairy Queen* (1692)

The progression vi–I (VI–i) should also be avoided because the tonal centre needs a stronger approach chord, such as V or IV. On the other hand, *roots falling a 3rd* are stronger because they generally move from the tonic (see 'Scale movements in the bass' above).

Progressions of first inversions. These may move freely up and down by step. They derive historically from later organum, which involved movement in first-inversion ($\frac{6}{3}$) chords.[4]

Palestrina: Mass, *Aeterna Christi Munera* (1590)

The scale movement in the following example creates a melodic rather than a harmonic sense of direction, although the 'floating' passage is brought down to earth harmonically by a strong cadence formula.

Weelkes: *When David heard* (c.1600)

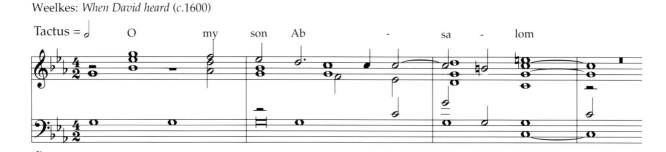

[4] Also called 'faux bourdon'

The first-inversion series forms a characteristic sequential pattern in the Baroque period:

Handel: *Dixit Dominus* (1707)

(Allegro)

Exercise

Realise this passage in four parts.

70 Handel: *Zadok the Priest* (1727)

(A tempo ordinario)

Al - le - lu - jah, Al - le - lu - jah, Al - le - lu - jah, A - men

(c) Weak progressions: the consecutives rule

The most difficult progressions to handle are those which rise or fall by step, e.g.: I–ii; V–vi (the interrupted cadence); vi–V; etc. These all involve the risk of consecutives unless there is some movement in contrary motion. Occurrences are to be found, particularly between inside parts, but the rule of *no* consecutives remained the general norm, since the bareness of the sound of the repeated 5th or 8ve with the same layout of parts was still unacceptable in this period. However, the consecutives rule applies only to moving parts and to perfect 5ths. The interval of a diminished 5th may be followed in the same parts by a perfect 5th and vice versa, except between the bass and any other part.

Stepwise root progressions, nevertheless, really belong to the modal period of the Renaissance and earlier, where movement towards a tonal centre was often lacking, or to the world of the late 19th-century Impressionists, where root movement by step was a characteristic trait:

Palestrina: Mass, *Aeterna Christi Munera* (1590)

Tactus = 𝅝

F:

Debussy: *Pour le Piano* (1901) Sarabande.
Avec un elegance grave et lente

E:

2. HARMONY AT THE CADENCE: SOME FURTHER CHARACTERISTICS

(a) The cadential $\frac{6}{4}$

During the Baroque period decorations other than the suspension became common at the cadence. The decorated dominant (Ic–V) became typical of the late Baroque and Classical styles, and decorations of the tonic (usually involving the progression I–IVc–I) also occurred:

Handel: *Messiah* (1742)

Larghetto

Ibid.

(A tempo ordinario)

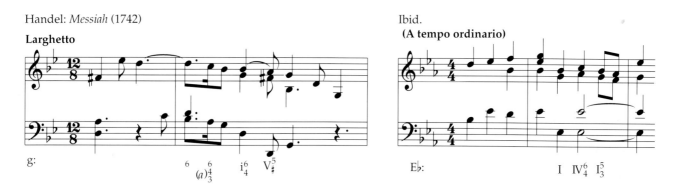

g:

^{6} $\underset{(a)}{^6_3}$ i^6_4 $V^5_{\sharp}$

Eb:

I IV^6_4 I^5_3

(A further use of the second inversion is as an unaccented passing chord, where the $\frac{6}{4}$ or $\frac{6}{3}$ occurs on a weak beat, moving by step, as at (*a*) in the first example above.)

Exercises

Identify the $\frac{6}{4}$ $\frac{5}{3}$ (Ic–V) progression in this cadence.

71 Handel: Suite No. 7 for Keyboard (*c.*1733)

c: Bb:*

* Hemiola — see p. 58

Complete in four parts for strings. Label the chords.

72 Geminiani: Concerto Grosso Op. 3 No. 6 (1732)

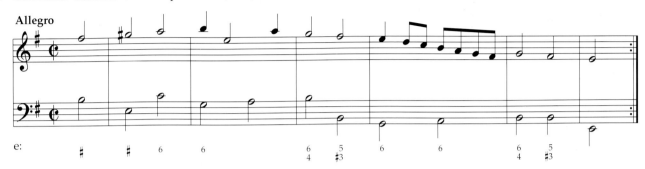

73 Handel: *Jephtha* (1751)

Complete the continuo part. Remember to allow the soloist freedom by avoiding doubling the melodic line.

74 Handel: Violin Sonata Op. 1 No. 13 (*c*.1730)

* Hemiola — see p. 58

75   Violin Sonata Op. 1 No. 6 (*c.*1730), attributed to Handel

Take down the bass part. Indicate the chords used with roman numerals.

76   Handel: *Messiah* (1742)

(b) Harmonic rhythm: the hemiola

It became increasingly common for the harmonic rhythm to quicken towards the cadence; this gave a forward momentum to the music.

Exercise

Label the chords in this passage, noting the rate of harmonic change. Fill in a part for the 2nd violin. (The original is in four parts.)

77   Purcell: *The Fairy Queen* (1692)

* Hemiola — see (b)

This effect was further enhanced by the use of the 'hemiola', a rhythmic interaction between the standard metre of the piece and the harmonic rhythm, creating a broadening at cadences:

Buxtehude: *Jesu, meine Freude* (c.1680)

The hemiola, with its syncopated effect, serves to drive home the message of the words in no uncertain manner. Sing this passage:

Handel: *Messiah* (1742)

Exercises

Bracket the hemiolas in the following examples and identify the chords, noting the progressions.

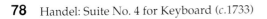

78 Handel: Suite No. 4 for Keyboard (c.1733)

79   Monteverdi: *Il ballo delle Ingrate* (1608)

80   Purcell: *The Fairy Queen* (1692)

Add a 2nd violin part, and label the chords. Begin by phrasing this longer extract and identifying the cadences.

81   Corelli: Concerto Grosso Op. 6 No. 4 (*c*.1711)

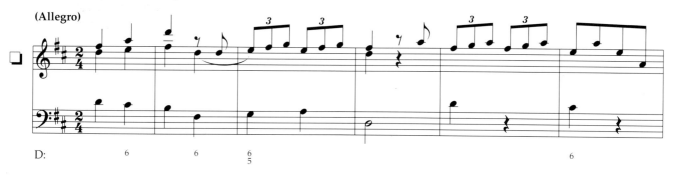

Take down the continuation of the 1st violin part; add the 2nd violin part, noting the figures.

82   Handel: Concerto Grosso Op. 6 No. 11 (1739)

(c) 'Coloured' chords at the cadence

The Baroque period saw the introduction of several chromatically altered or 'coloured' chords before the dominant. These included the diminished 7th and Neapolitan 6th chords.

(i) *The diminished 7th chord (vii^{d7}).* Chords with a dominant function include V, V^7, vii (diminished triad), vii^7, and vii^{d7}; their normal resolution is to the tonic triad:

As may be seen, the diminished 7th chord is built up in minor 3rds on the semitone below the root of the chord of resolution. In music of the 17th and 18th centuries it usually occurs in the minor key, where its characteristic sound adds to the expressiveness of the passage involved:

D. Scarlatti: Sonata in F minor, Kp. 481, L. 187 (1720–55)

Exercise

Identify the diminished 7ths.

83   Bach: Fantasia in G minor BWV 542 (1717-23)

The diminished 7th may also appear as a decoration of the supertonic ($\sharp i^{d7}$) or dominant ($\sharp iv^{d7}$) chord:

Bach: Prelude and Fugue No. 7, '48', Book 2 (1742)

Exercise

Complete in five parts.

84   Bach: 'Fecit potentiam', *Magnificat* (1723 revised c.1728)

(He hath scattered the proud in the imagination of their hearts)

The diminished 7th may appear in a modulating sequence.

Exercises

Bracket the modulations.

85 Bach: Prelude No. 12, '48', Book 2 (1742)

86 Bach: Prelude No. 14, '48', Book 2 (1742)

(ii) *The Neapolitan 6th (♭IIb).* This chord took its name from its frequent use by Alessandro Scarlatti (1660–1725), who composed operas for many years in Naples. It is a major chord, built on the flattened supertonic. In music of the 17th and 18th centuries it is usually found in the minor key in its first inversion, hence the term 'Neapolitan 6th'. (For its use in the 19th century, see Chapter 7.) It functions in the same way as iib, moving towards V directly (*a*), via ic (*b*), or via a diminished 7th chord (*c*):

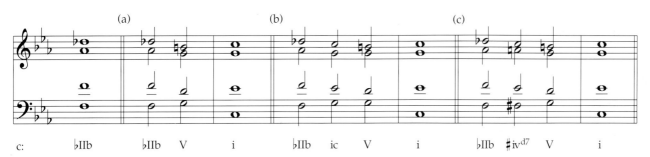

Exercise

87 Write out Neapolitan 6th chords with different resolutions in the minor keys of c, g, d, and a.

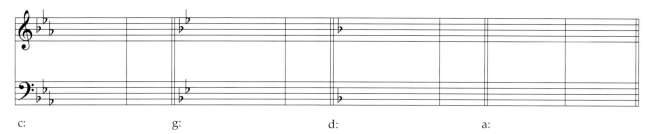

Notice how effectively Handel sets these desolate words, and the role played by the 'coloured' chords just before the cadence.

Handel: *Messiah* (1742)

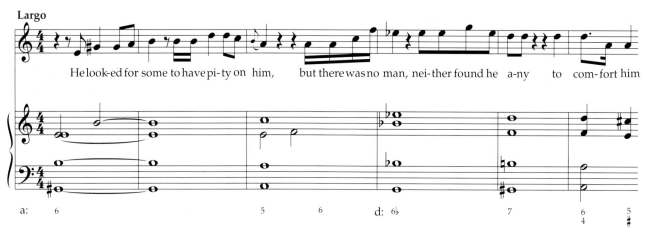

Exercises

Complete the figured bass in four string parts and indicate the chords used. Note the hemiolas.

88 Purcell: Canzona from *The Fairy Queen* (1692)

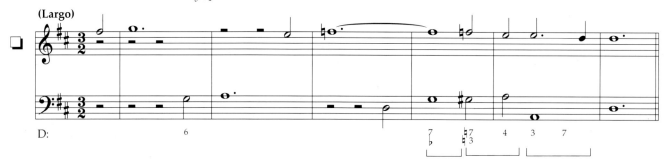

89 J. Stanley: Violin Sonata in G minor (? 1740)

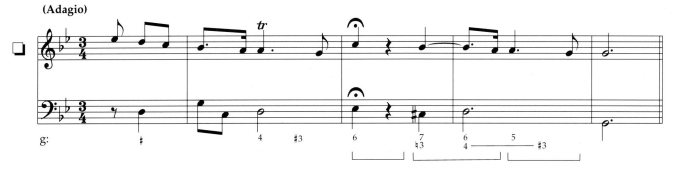

(d) The plagal cadence (IV–I)

This lacks the drive of the perfect cadence and may occur as a phrase ending in the course of a piece, rather than as the final cadence, unless it is added as an 'Amen'.

Este's Psalter (1592)

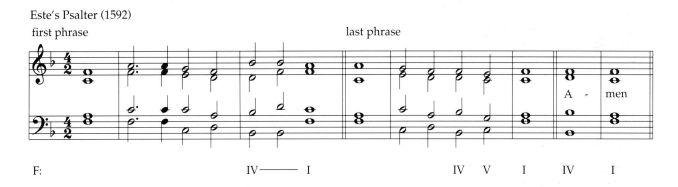

The closing bars of Handel's anthem *Zadok the Priest* consist of a repetition of the plagal formula.

Exercise

Label the chords.

90 Handel: *Zadok the Priest* (1727)

Frequently the plagal cadence is used at the end of a 'pedal' passage, usually a cadential extension in itself, during which the music may hover round IVc or suggest a modulation to the key of chord IV. Pedal notes, over or under which harmonies dissonant to them may pass, often serve to apply a 'brake' to the music:

Bach: R. 143

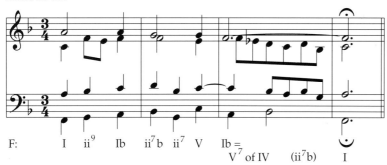

F: I   ii⁹   Ib   ii⁷b   ii⁷   V   Ib =   I
                                                        V⁷ of IV   (ii⁷b)

3. MODULATION

Modulation is the changing from one key to another in the course of a composition. It is a vital feature of tonal music in pieces of any length, where to remain in the same key would almost certainly spell harmonic monotony. Key relationships are a basic and often exciting aspect of composition, and a composer's method and timing of key change is crucial. A modulation may be a dramatic stroke (*a*) or a transient excursion (*b*); many are so smooth that the change of tonal centre is almost imperceptible, while some provide a special 'moment' for performer and listener.

(*a*) Bach: *St Matthew Passion* (1729) (outline)

(Vivace)

G:

F♯:

(*b*) Bach: R. 136

G: e: x   G:
                                x

Key relationships

These fall into two categories, viz.:

(i) *The closely related keys*. These include the keys of the primary triads (I, IV, and V) and their relative minors or majors, giving the tonic and five closely related keys in all. The following diagram shows the keys closely related to C major and minor.

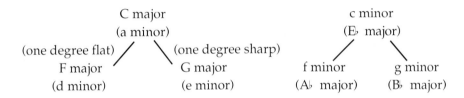

(ii) *The remote or foreign keys*. These include all the other keys. A modulation to a remote key in the period 1600–1850 might well have a considerable impact, but distant modulations became the norm in the later 19th century as the use of chromatic harmony increased.

Whatever means are used to effect a modulation, a chord of the dominant group, V, V^7, viib, or vii^{d7}, is usually needed to establish the new key, either at the point of modulation, or, if it is an abrupt change, fairly soon into the new key. (See the examples below.)

Methods of changing key

(i) Modulation may be accomplished by the use of a *pivot* or *'ambiguous' chord* (or chords) i.e. one which is common both to the old and new keys, followed by the establishment of the new key in the accepted way, via the dominant, dominant 7th, viib, or vii^{d7}.

Croft: 'St Anne' (*c*.1708)

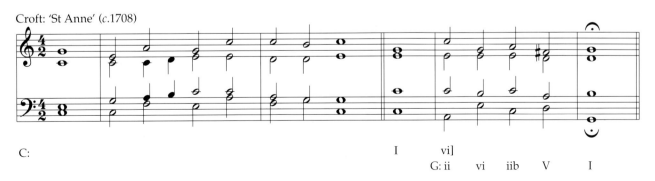

C:

                                         I   vi]

                                      G: ii   vi   iib   V   I

(ii) Occasionally modulation is effected simply by the use of a pivot *note*, e.g. a note of the tonic chord can be held over; the next chord placed under or over it then 'takes over', and the music proceeds in the new key.

Bach: R. 251

(iii) Modulation may also be accomplished by a leap or abrupt change; a phrase may simply start in a new key, seemingly ignoring the previous cadence. Sometimes called 'phrase modulation', this is a frequent occurrence in Bach's chorale harmonizations:

Bach: R. 74

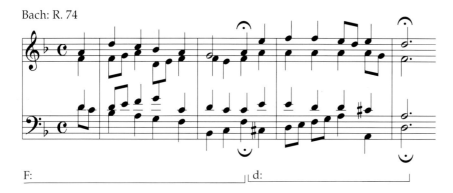

Similarly, an effective change in key colour is often apparent between one movement and the next; see the following example:

Handel: *Messiah* (1742)

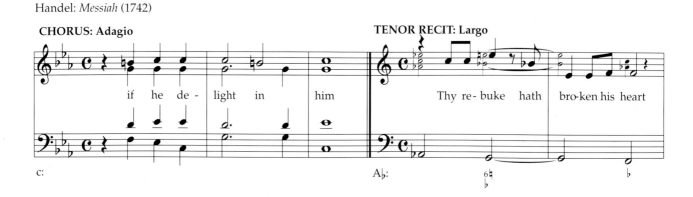

(iv) A chromatic move in the bass is another favourite device for modulation.

Bach: 'Esurientes', *Magnificat* (1723 revised c.1728)

(v) From the early Baroque onwards 'modulation' by sequence was a common method of key change. The sequence in the following example includes three overlapping statements of a melody.

Bach: *Jesu, meine Freude* (?1723)

(vi) The switch from the tonic major to the tonic minor added another dimension of colour; this was to be more common in the music of Schubert and Brahms, but had its roots in the Baroque. In the following extract the 'echo', a popular Baroque trait, moves into the minor with telling effect.

Exercises

Listen to this example and bracket the key change.

91 Violin Sonata Op. 1 No. 11 (*c*.1730), attributed to Handel

Identify the modulations.

92 Purcell: *Jehora, quam multi sunt hostes mei* (c. 1680)

E - go cu - bui et dor - mi - vi; e - go ex - per - ge fe - ci me; et dor-

mi - vi et dor - mi - vi; ex - per - ge fe - ci me;

(I lay me down and slept, then I awaked)

93 Purcell: Fantazia No. 2 in Four Parts (1680)

4. THE USE OF DISSONANCE

In the Baroque period the expressive qualities of dissonance were explored still further, especially in Germany, where contrapuntal complexity and emotional intensity went hand in hand.

(a) The suspension

The role of the suspension in the Baroque differed little from that in the Renaissance. Its chief function was to create a sense of movement and drive through syncopation, particularly at the cadence bars. The dissonance might appear as either a tied or a repeated note from a weak to a strong(er) beat. In slow music the suspension served to pull back the music, extracting the most from every chord; where words were involved this was most effective.

Exercises

Sing or play the following two passages. Figure the suspensions and dominant 7ths.

94   Bach: *St Matthew Passion* (1729)

g:

((The griefs) how bitter, yet how sweet are they!)

Observe how the chord spacing at X enhances the poignancy of the extract from Handel's *Messiah* below.

95   Handel: *Messiah* (1742)

*   c:

He was wounded for our transgressions, he was bruised for our iniquities!

Complete these organ voluntaries by John Stanley in two parts. Suspensions frequently occur in the sequences, producing a characteristic Baroque effect.

96   Vol. 1 No. 1 (1748)

a:

* Modal key signature

97   Vol. 1 No. 5 (1748)

D:

98   Vol. 2 No. 1 (1752)

d:

Figure the suspensions in this passage.

99   Handel: *Semele* (1743)

f:

(The death of Semele)

Double suspensions were quite common: figure these in the example below. Sing
the passage, noting the madrigalian word-setting.

100 Purcell: *Dido and Aeneas* (1689)

Complete the bass part of this organ voluntary in three parts, noting the double
suspensions.

101 J. Stanley: Organ Voluntary Vol. 1 No. 1 (1748)

Complete a four-part harmonization of the opening of Dido's Lament.[4] Sing it
through. Mark the suspensions with 'X'.

102 Purcell: *Dido and Aeneas* (1689)

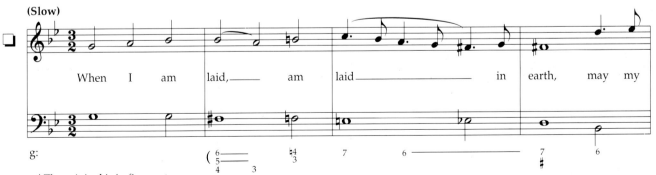

[4] The original is in five parts.

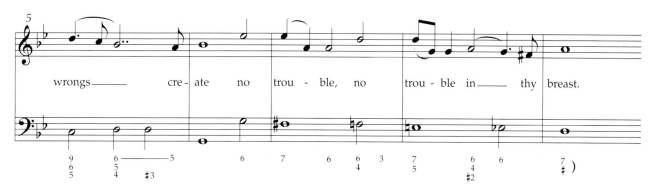

Complete this 'Prelude for the Witches'. Mark the suspensions.

103 Ibid.

(b) Unprepared dissonance

(i) *The accented passing note.* This was frequently used in contrapuntal music, where its dissonant quality aided the momentum of the music. Accented passing notes often occurred in pairs on the weaker beats, especially in the music of Purcell and Corelli.

Exercise

Ring the accented passing notes in the following passage.

104 Violin Sonata Op. 1 No. 15 (*c.*1730), attributed to Handel

(ii) *The appoggiatura (or 'leaning note')*. This decoration originated in vocal music, where initially it functioned in a similar way to the accented passing note, taking the strong beat and principal time allowance away from its resolution. However, in the hands of Monteverdi and the early opera writers, it became freed of such constraints and was exploited for its ability to arrest the ear, by leaping on to a dissonance. The use of this dissonance increased in the 18th century. It remained prominent in recitative, serving the words, especially at phrase endings, and was frequently added as an unscripted ornament. It was the appoggiatura's power of expression, particularly of grief and anguish, which ensured its popularity with composers.

The following examples by Bach and Handel show the expressive use of the appoggiatura.

Bach: Cantata No. 21, *Ich hatte viel Bekümmernis* (?1713)

'Sobs, tears, sorrow, need; sobs, tears, fearful longing'

Exercises

Ring the appoggiaturas and note their effect in the following extracts.

105   Bach: *St Matthew Passion* (1729)

106   Handel: Concerto Grosso Op. 6 No. 4 (1739)

5. CHROMATIC WRITING

Although the late Renaissance had produced several composers active in the search for expression through chromaticism (see p. 22) it was not until later in the Baroque that this feature was systematized through the gradual establishment of tonality and key. Vicentino's micro-tonal experiments gave way ultimately to an acceptance of 'equal temperament', and it was the establishment of this that opened up further harmonic possibilities; composers could now write in, and modulate to, any key. These possibilities were fully realized by the composers of the late Baroque, especially Bach, in pieces like the Chromatic Fantasy and Fugue and the Ricercar à 6 from the *Musical Offering*:

Bach: Ricercar à 6 from the *Musical Offering* (1747)

The musical language of these instrumental pieces is serious and eloquent; the effect of the same language is intensified when allied to words.

Exercises

Sing these passages and comment on this language in the three examples below, under the following headings:

  (a) chromatic writing,
  (b) dissonance,
  (c) rhythmic character.

107 Purcell: Lament from *Dido and Aeneas* (1689)

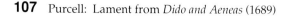

108 Handel: *Utrecht Te Deum* (1713)

(Adagio)

(*p*)

When Thou hast o - ver - come the sharp - ness of death, the sharp - ness, the sharp - ness of death, of death.

a:

109 Bach: *St Matthew Passion* (1729)

(Allegro)

b: Let Him be   cru   -   -   (ci–fied,)

3. Baroque Style:
The Chorale

The importance of the chorale lies in the central position it holds in German music of the Baroque period. The evolution of the chorale began with Martin Luther (1483–1546), one of the founders of German Protestantism. Luther considered the chorale or hymn a vital component of Church worship, and spent much time in building a repertory of suitable texts and melodies; Neumeister, Franck, Nicolai, Picander, and Luther himself were among the 'poets' who contributed words, which were in the vernacular so that ordinary people could 'sing with understanding'. For the music Luther used pre-Reformation hymns and plainsong melodies, such as 'Veni Redemptor', which became 'Nun komm, der Heiden Heiland' (R. 28). He even adapted secular folk- and popular songs of earlier times; for example, 'O Haupt voll Blut und Wunden' was originally a love-song by H. Hassler.

1524 saw the publication of J. Walther's Songbook, the first of many collections of chorales. Luther himself composed 36 chorales including 'Ein' feste Burg'; other composers include J. Cruger (e.g. 'Jesu, meine Freude' and 'Herzliebster Jesu'), M. Vulpius, H. Isaac, M. Praetorius and P. Nicolai, who often wrote both words and music (e.g. 'Wachet auf').

The 17th century showed continued activity in the writing of chorale melodies together with their use as a basis of composition. Cantatas, oratorios, and Passions of the late 17th and early 18th centuries include many examples of chorales, both 'straight' for congregational participation, and in elaborate settings; see, for example, the opening choruses of Bach's *St Matthew Passion* and Cantata No. 140, *Wachet auf*.

The Chorale Prelude

It became the custom in the Lutheran Church for the chorale that was to be sung by the congregation to be played on the organ before the service. From simple beginnings this quickly developed into an art form in its own right, affording rich examples of contrapuntal skill, notably in the hands of D. Buxtehude (*c*.1637–1707), J. Pachelbel (1653–1706), and J. S. Bach (1685–1750). Bach wrote about 140 chorale preludes, which are to be found in various collections including the *Orgelbüchlein* (1717) — a most useful collection for examining different treatments of chorale melodies.

Subsequent Use of the Chorale

Later composers of chorale preludes include Brahms, Reger, and Karg-Elert, whilst Mendelssohn used the chorale 'Vater unser im Himmelreich' in his Sixth Organ

Sonata. The chorale is also found in Hindemith's *Mathis der Maler*, R. Vaughan Williams' *Hodie* and Britten's *Noye's Fludde* and *St Nicholas*.

The Melody Line of the Chorale

Since many chorale melodies have their roots in plainsong, they are generally simple with stepwise movement. Jumps in the melody usually occur at the beginning, and in between phrases. Repeated notes are common.

The chorale, as Bach inherited it, had become a strong, forthright tune in a regular metre. $\frac{4}{4}$ time was the most common, although there are some examples of $\frac{3}{4}$ time. It reflected the Lutheran spirit of solidarity and proud faith. The frequent cadences, indicated by a pause sign ⌢, supported and strengthened the structure, together with basic harmony that usually changed on the crotchet beat, i.e. with every syllable sung. The following are typical phrases from chorales.

R. 20, 'Ein' feste Burg'[1]

D:

R. 74, 'O Haupt voll Blut und Wunden'

F:

Repeated notes are common:
R. 32, 'Nun danket alle Gott'

A:

Luther adapted plainsong melodies, which are frequently modal in character:
R. 28, 'Nun komm, der Heiden Heiland'

b:

Exercise

110 Write out, sing, play, and memorize some chorale melodies. They may be seen in context in Bach's *St Matthew Passion*.

---

[1] R. = number in A. Riemenschneider, *371 Harmonized Chorales and 69 Chorale Melodies with Figured Bass by J. S. Bach* (London, Schirmer, 1941).

The Harmonic Characteristics of Bach's Chorale Settings

1. GENERAL COMMENTS

The harmony is usually of the basic, functional kind, using primary triads and their inversions, often in the progression of 5ths, and modulating to closely related keys. The importance of the chorale as an art form lies in the way Bach treats this basic harmony: frequently there is an almost overwhelming profusion of contrapuntal and harmonic decoration, which makes the form unique.

Exercises

Play these examples and label the chords.

As well as the progression of 5ths, chords with roots dropping a 3rd, towards the cadence, are strong:

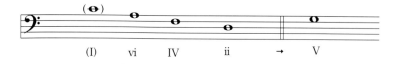

(See also R. 23 and 32)

2. THE CADENCE

Since the cadence bars constitute at least one third of a chorale, they are perhaps its most characteristic feature, and they need careful consideration.

(a) General points

(i) Suspensions do not occur on the pause chord, as a general rule; but see R. 141 and 279 as exceptions.

(ii) Passing notes do not occur between a pause chord and the next phrase, on account of the lack of words.

(iii) The leading note will often fall a 3rd to the 5th of the triad, thus creating the sonority of a complete chord. It may also *rise* to the 3rd of the tonic chord.

(iv) The final chord of the chorale is always major.

(v) With a few exceptions (see p. 91), the cadence chords are in root position.

(b) The perfect cadence

There are several melodic forms of this cadence, to which Bach applies two basic formulae with variations.

(i) Frequently chord V is preceded by ii^7 b:

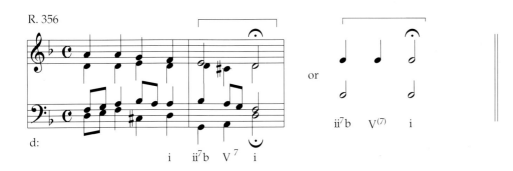

(ii) The other basic formula uses the Renaissance 4–3 suspension over chord V:

Exercise

114 Identify the progressions in the following example and complete for S.A.T.B.

G:

(c) The cadential $\frac{6}{4}$

Exercises

115 Label the cadence chords.   **116**

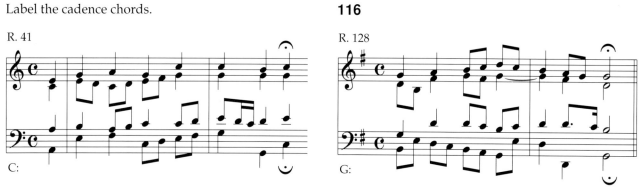

R. 41   R. 128

C: G:

Bach uses the $\frac{6}{4}$ on the 2nd beat of the bar in $\frac{3}{4}$ time, often creating a hemiola effect (see p. 58):

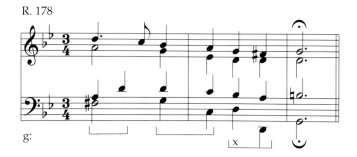

R. 178

g:

He occasionally doubles the 6th rather than the bass note in the $\frac{6}{4}$ chord. As with his doubled major 3rds, the two parts move in contrary motion:

R. 171

F:

Although the cadential $\begin{smallmatrix}6\\4\end{smallmatrix}$ is found occasionally, one has the feeling that more often Bach actually avoids using it when he could do so.

Exercises

117 Label the cadence chords in these examples.   **118**

R. 166

g:*

R. 168

*   c:

(d) Other perfect cadence patterns

(i) *Chord ii⁷*. Although chord ii⁷b is more frequently found before V at the cadence, chord ii in root position sometimes occurs, especially in the major key. (It is a diminished triad in the minor key.) Bach usually prepares the 7th. The *sound* is very different from that of ii⁷b.

R. 179

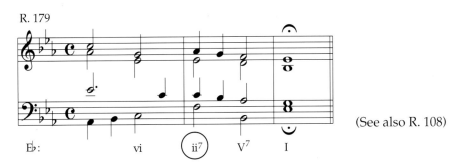

Eb: vi   ii⁷   V⁷   I

(See also R. 108)

(ii) *Chord IV⁷*. Chord IV⁷ may also occur before V at the cadence. The 7th is frequently unprepared though it usually moves down by step. In the example below notice: (*a*) the doubled major 3rds (x) in the first bar, including the doubled leading note, both approached by contrary motion; (*b*) the 5th falling in chord IV⁷ (bar 2) to avoid consecutives; (*c*) the sensitive approach to V⁷ in the penultimate chord (⌐).

R. 14

G: x   x   IVb   IV⁷   V₄   ⁷₃   I

* Modal key signature

(iii) *Chord IIIb*. Cadences using IIIb are to be avoided, as they are rare:

R. 3

a:*   III⁺b

(iv) *Modulation to the subdominant key*. This may be implied by the unusual cadential formula of a falling 3rd in the melody.

Exercises

Label the cadence bars.

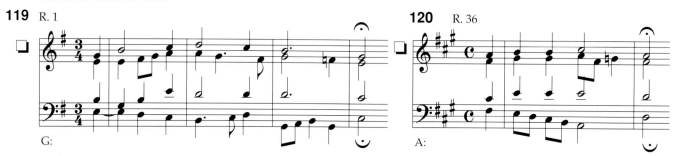

119   R. 1

G:

120   R. 36

A:

Work these examples.

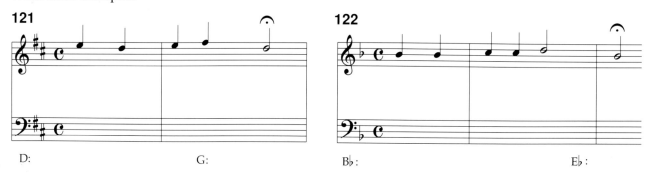

121

D: G:

122

B♭:   E♭:

Work these examples of perfect cadences for S.A.T.B.

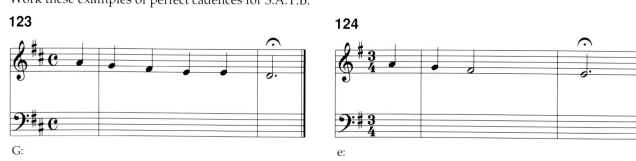

123

G:

124

e:

* Modal key signature

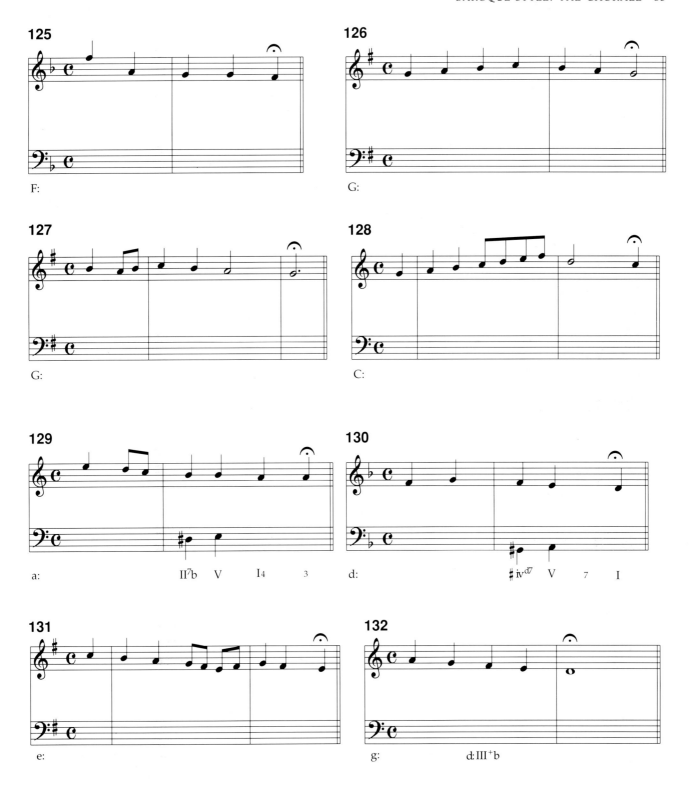

(e) The imperfect cadence

The 'half close' occurs at least once in the course of a chorale and is almost as strong as the perfect cadence (full close). It is often not resolved—either the next phrase will start in another key (a), or the half close constitutes the final cadence, as is generally the case in modal chorales (b):

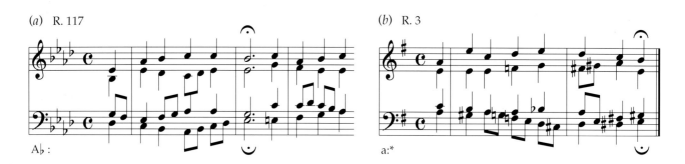

Bach frequently contrives a strong running bass in contrary motion at the half close.

Exercises

Label the cadence chords.

Work these examples of imperfect cadences for S.A.T.B.

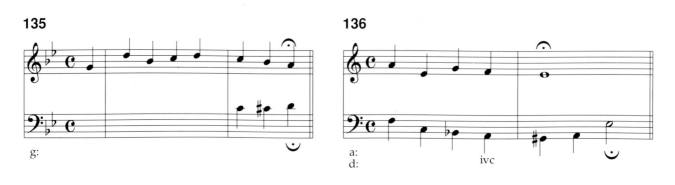

* Modal key signature

(f) The interrupted cadence

Some of Bach's most dramatic moments in the chorale are the interrupted cadences.
They are very rare, but may occur in a long chorale or in one with short phrases,
placed near the end to avoid two consecutive perfect cadences in the same key (a).
Example (b) must be a musical exclamation mark!

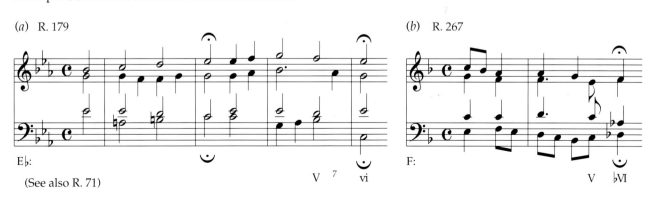

* Modal key signature

Exercises

Complete the harmony for S.A.T.B. in the following examples. Note the modulation
to the key of chord iii at x.

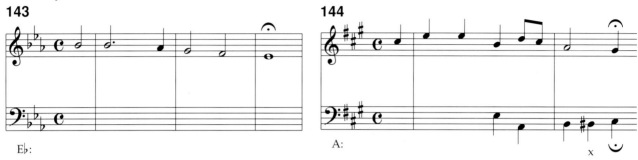

(g) The plagal cadence

Plagal cadences are almost as rare as interrupted cadences.

They usually form cadential extensions, preceded by some form of perfect cadence.
Bach will often *modulate* to chord IV to strengthen the progression, and decorate it
with contrapuntal lines. Note the use of the minor chord iv in this impressive
example:

Exercises

Complete the following examples for S.A.T.B, then copy in Bach's workings from
Riemenschneider and compare the two.

146   R. 283

e:

147   Take down the lower parts as an aural exercise.

F:

3. THE DOMINANT 7th CHORD

Although not bound by the strict conventions of the Renaissance, which demanded
preparation of the 7th as a dissonance, Bach still treats the dominant 7th chord with
great care, particularly in root position, where it is usually prepared, introduced in
stepwise movement, or treated as a passing note :

In some cases the chord is the highlight of a phrase:

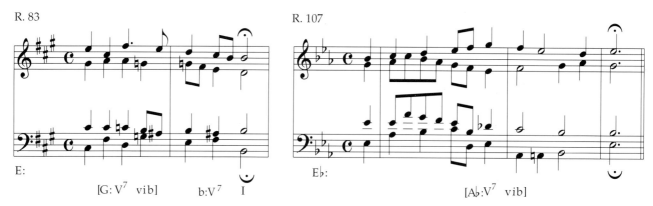

(a) V⁷ in first inversion (V⁷b)

This is a common form of V⁷. In the following example from R. 244, note the crossing of parts for 'horizontal' interest:

V⁷b often follows IVb, in which the 7th is prepared (*a*). To avoid consecutives, the 3rd may be doubled in IVb, with the harmony changing on the quaver beat (*b*). Bach sometimes enhances IVb with a prepared 7th to great effect (*c*).

R. 83

A:

V^7b also frequently effects an abrupt modulation from one phrase to another:

R. 80

R. 158

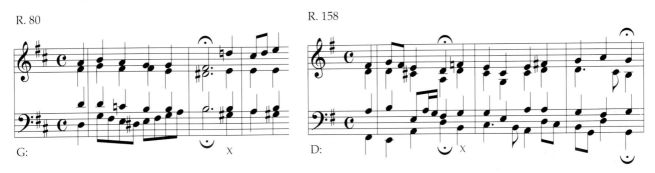

G:

D:

A rare but striking cadence is one in which the last chord is V^7b. This may suggest
an unusual modulation.

R. 216

R. 61

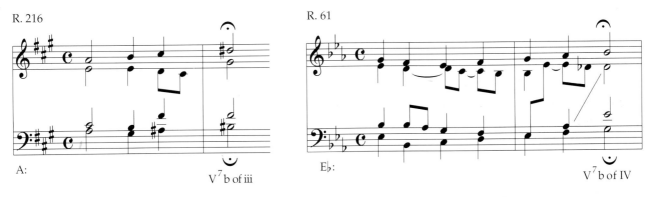

A:

V^7b of iii

E♭:

V^7b of IV

R. 78

D:

V^7b of v

(b) V^7 in second inversion (V^7c)

This chord is rarely used. Bach will generally opt for the passing $^6_3$ (VIIb): V^7c makes a passing modulation into A♭ at x in R. 107; notice also a rare use of chord iii in bar 1.

(c) V^7 in third inversion (V^7d)

The last inversion is frequently employed, especially at the beginning of a phrase, to give a forward-moving impetus to the harmony because of the downward movement of the 7th. Notice the outstanding tenor part in R. 50. Bach's tenor lines are a notable feature of the chorale, frequently providing a counter melody:

Exercises

Complete these phrases using the appropriate V^7 chord at x.

4. THE DIMINISHED 7th CHORD (d^7)

The diminished 7th chord is generally found in the minor key as a substitute for V^7b.
It always adds a degree of tension to the music and is often part of a dramatic
modulating passage:

It also acts as a 'coloured' chord at the cadence; here as an altered version of iv^7 —
(the diminished 7th of the dominant key)[2]:

[2] See p.62.

Exercises

Identify the diminished 7ths in the following passages; onto which chords do they resolve?

Write in diminished 7th chords and their resolutions at x and R.

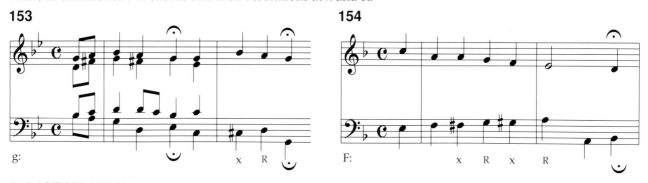

5. MODULATION

Bach will usually modulate at least once in a chorale; most chorales contain several modulations, either *en passant* or at the cadence points. Frequently the new key is introduced at or near the beginning of a phrase, then firmly established at the succeeding cadence:

Chords V, V⁷ and viib and the diminished 7th chord are all used by Bach to modulate (iiib is rarely used). Frequently there is an abrupt modulation from one phrase to the next:

R. 24

Some very effective passing modulations occur *within* the phrase; notice the melodic tenor line in this example:

R. 107

The flattened 7th chord is sometimes used to 'contradict' a modulation:

R. 36

Exercises

Add an alto part to the following two chorales, noting the modulations.

155 'Ich liebe Jesum alle Stund'

156 'Komm, süsser Tod'

Add a bass part: indicate the modulations.

157 'Gib dich zufrieden'

c:*

6. 'CONTRAPUNTAL HARMONY'

(a) The treatment of dissonance and unessential notes

Bach's use of dissonance in the form of suspensions and accented passing notes, together with passing or auxiliary notes and the occasional anticipation note, creates the texture which is such a distinctive feature of the chorale style; a glance through Riemenschneider will confirm this. The moving bass, in particular, adds strength and character to the harmonizations:

R. 9

G:

* Modal key signature

(i) *The suspension.* Both crotchets and quavers are used as suspensions. These may occur on any beat of the bar, and often as a chain. Bass suspensions provide rhythmic interest.

Exercises

Play these extracts and figure the suspensions.

158 R. 152

159 R. 238

160 R. 147

161 Continue these chains of suspensions and complete in four parts.

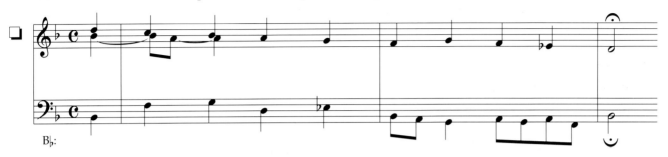

162 Realize the figured bass in this passage, which includes a rare example of a double suspension.

163 Complete these passages, filling in the figured suspensions.

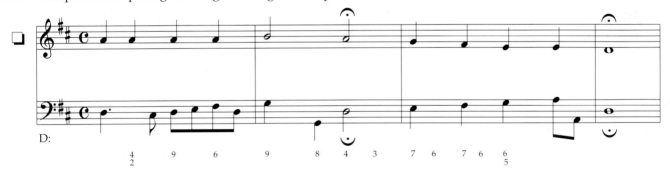

164 Add suspensions to the chords marked x.

165

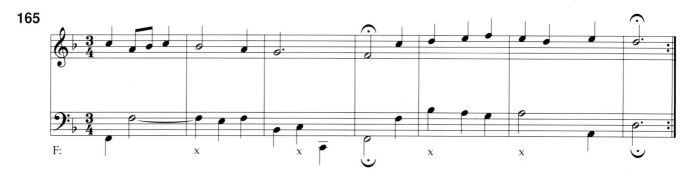

166 Complete these passages, which include bass suspensions.

167

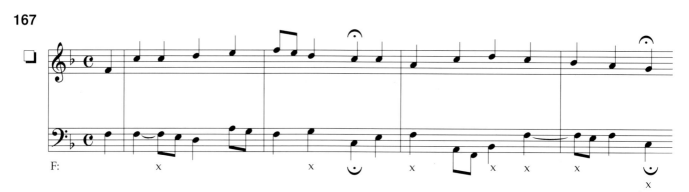

(ii) *Accented passing notes.* Accented passing notes generally occur as quavers. They are more usually found in descending passages, but there are also many ascending examples. As in music of the Renaissance period, accented passing notes usually occur on the weaker beats of the bar:

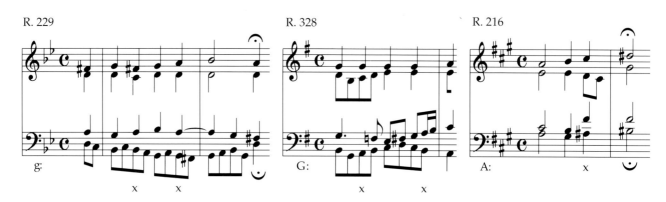

Exercise

168 Harmonize this passage, which contains accented passing notes.

(b) The moving bass

Bach's flowing basses are a mixture of passing and harmony notes, consisting of scale and arpeggio movement and 8ve leaps. The bass is frequently shadowed by movement in 10ths and 3rds in the other parts. When there is an abundance of quaver movement a quickening of the harmonic rhythm often results, with the harmony (particularly at the cadence) changing on the quaver beat. Bass patterns often move in sequences:

R. 34

R. 8

Exercises

169 Label the chords in the following passage.

Notice how Bach treats repeated notes and scale passages in the melody lines of these extracts. Add the inner parts (alto and tenor).

170   **171**

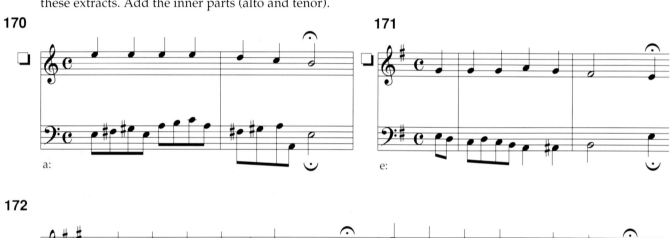

172

173

(c) The anticipation note

This usually occurs at the cadence:

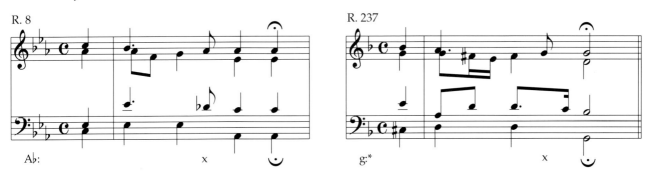

Consecutive 5ths are not uncommon between the anticipation note and the dominant 7th note, usually between the soprano and tenor parts: this was a traditional procedure that Bach chose to retain.

Exercises

174 Add a flowing bass part to the following chorale.

'Gott, wie gross ist deine Güte'

* Modal key signature

175   Take down the bass as an aural exercise.

'Jesu ist das schönste Licht'

7. THE PART-WRITING

(a) Consecutives

Bach followed the convention of his day and generally avoided consecutives, sometimes making use of the suspension to do so:

R. 297

The chorales include a few examples of consecutives which he probably just overlooked. However, he evidently found acceptable consecutive 5ths involved with the anticipation note (see above).

(b) Crossing of parts

This is a frequent occurrence; the tenor line, which is consistently in a high register, often soars above the alto part, and sometimes moves below the bass, which is duplicated an 8ve lower by the accompaniment:

R. 56

e:

(See also R. 50, p. 92.)

A sense of freedom pervades part-movement in the choral, with each voice having an independent life of its own.

(c) Doubled major 3rds

Major 3rds are doubled frequently; the parts involved will usually move in contrary motion.

Exercises

Identify the doubled 3rds in the extracts below.

176   R. 6   177   R. 6

F: F: (!)

8. THE PASSING $\frac{6}{4}$ AND $\frac{6}{3}$

Bach uses both $\frac{6}{4}$ and $\frac{6}{3}$ as passing chords, but generally favours the latter (the passing $\frac{6}{4}$ is more characteristic of the later Classical period):

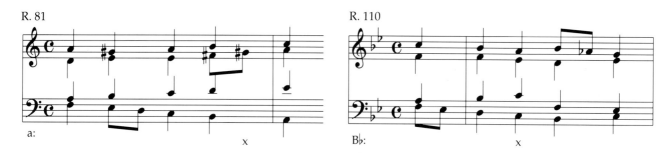

In the chorale the passing $\frac{6}{4}$ will most frequently appear as a chord ic on the last or weak beat of the bar, in between chords ivb and ii⁷b, with parts moving step by step:

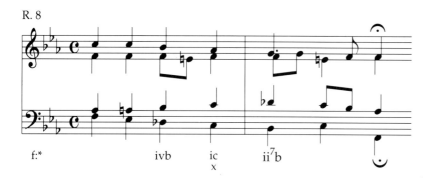

Note, in the following example, that however the passing $\frac{6}{4}$ is presented, the part-writing will always be smooth:

* Modal key signature

Exercises

Fill in the appropriate $\frac{6}{4}$ or $\frac{6}{3}$ chord at x.

178

b:

179

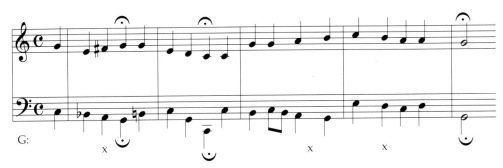

G:

9. CHROMATIC MOVEMENT

Chromatic passages in chorales are relatively rare; they occur when the 'affection' of the words demands this treatment, as in Bach's *St Matthew* and *St John* Passions. Although this harmony is most striking, it is certainly not the norm.

Play these examples:

R. 310: Bach: *St John Passion* (1724)

E:

Hadst Thou disdain'd this bondage sore, We had been bound for ever more.

Note the effective use of suspensions in the high tenor and alto parts in the first phrase, and the effect of the chromaticism in the second phrase.

Cantata No. 60, *O Ewigkeit, du Donnerwort* (1723), concludes with the chorale 'Es ist genug', in which the soul is resigned to death. Note how Bach matches the music to

the words in the extract below. The same harmonization is used by Alban Berg in his
Violin Concerto (1935).

R. 216

E:

My cares and troubles all behind me

Exercises

Complete these phrases for S.A.T.B. Note that notes chromatically raised (♯) in the
bass often become new leading notes, while notes chromatically lowered (♭) may
change the harmony from a major to a minor chord.

180

a:

181

e:

Take down the bass-line and complete for S.A.T.B.

182

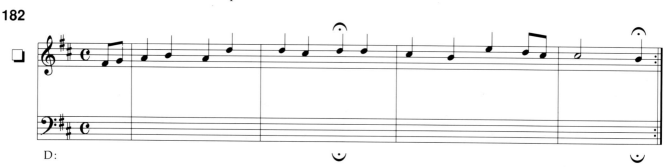

D:

183

g:

10. UNUSUAL CHORDS

In Bach's chorales the chord of the augmented triad (III⁺b), which is so common in
the music of Purcell, occurs only rarely, as does the chord of the Neapolitan 6th.

Exercises

Play the passages below and identify these chords.

184 Bach: *St Matthew Passion* (1729)   **185** R. 13

f: d:

186 R. 203   **187** R. 110

g:*   f:

188 R. 262

g:*

* Modal key signature

11. MODAL CHORALES

(*a*) Many of the melodies which Bach harmonized in his characteristic manner are modal in origin. Dorian, Mixolydian, and Aeolian are treated as D minor, G major, and A minor (or transposed equivalents of these). Chorales in the Phrygian mode, with its characteristic cadence F♯–E, end with an *imperfect cadence* in A minor, which is usually extended:

R. 352

C:

(*b*) The *key signature* is often the clue to a modal chorale (see Chapter 1, p.5). Note that D minor, therefore, may have no key signature (see R. 49, 80, 185), G minor only one flat (R. 174), C minor only two flats (R.10), and F minor only three flats (R. 8). A minor may have one sharp, i.e. as the Dorian mode transposed *up* a 5th (R. 3).

(*c*) The *flattened leading note* is often present in the first phrase of a modal chorale. It may lead to a modulation to the relative major or dominant key.

Exercises

Study Bach's treatment of the flattened leading note in these examples, and fill in the alto and tenor parts.

189   **190**

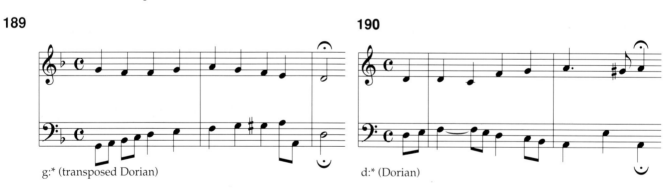

g:* (transposed Dorian)   d:* (Dorian)

* Modal key signature

Exercises

Complete the following modal chorales for S.A.T.B.

191

g:* (transposed Dorian)

192

a: (transposed Dorian)

* Modal key signature

4. Baroque Style: Two- and Three-part Counterpoint

Theorists of the Renaissance had drawn up strict rules on the writing of polyphony, music in which the melodic value of each part was of prime importance. Methods varied from the addition of a part or parts to an original 'cantus firmus' to the use of imitative polyphony in which the same theme (or themes) was used in every part. Broadly speaking, church music followed conservative, i.e. polyphonic, lines, whereas the secular madrigal, for example, more often mixed polyphony and homophonic writing, depending on the character of the words.

Baroque counterpoint falls into two main categories:

(i) Fugal polyphony, which is a combination of equal melodic parts: Bach's fugues combine strict contrapuntal practice with elaborate figuration to produce eloquent masterpieces.

(ii) A type of freer tonal counterpoint supported by the continuo in which the parts may have varying functions. A good example of this 'concertante' type of writing is the opening chorus of Cantata No. 140, *Wachet auf* (Sleepers Wake), where Bach combines at least four contrasting lines to produce an impressive web of sound. Although this music is contrapuntal, the presence of the continuo gives it a strong harmonic basis. (See page 113 opposite).

Baroque counterpoint is characterized by a rich abundance of figuration and motifs of instrumental origin. Many of Bach's choruses (such as the opening chorus of the *St Matthew Passion*) are enormous contrapuntal tapestries, which generally sustain the same textures throughout the movement and are based on ritornello structures.[1] On the other hand, much exciting music is a mixture of grand harmonic statements, fugal sections, and contrasted writing between voices and instruments — a style frequently found in Handel's great choruses.

One of the most satisfying aspects of playing and listening to Baroque music is this obsession with patterns of figuration, sequences, and part-writing of amazing complexity. The counterpoint is often allied to a basic pulse or 'beat', which is established at the beginning and retained to the end of a movement, filling it with energy and *joie de vivre*. Listen, for example, to the opening of Bach's Third Brandenburg Concerto, the fugal allegros in Handel's Op. 6 (concerti grossi), or the splendour of voices and instruments in the chorus quoted on p. 113 from Bach's Cantata No. 140.

---

[1] Ritornello form involves the recurrence of the opening tutti, sometimes in different keys, with episodes in between.

Bach: Cantata No. 140, *Wachet auf* (1731)

The Working of Counterpoint

Many of the following extracts contain the elements mentioned above, some in
miniature. Working the exercises should help to give the student some insight into
the fascinating world of Baroque counterpoint.

The following hints may prove useful:

   Always sing or play through the given part.

If there is no phrasing, pin-point the cadences first and note the modulations.

Use the given part to provide the maximum help in the working-out by asking the following questions.

1. *What type of counterpoint is involved?*

If the counterpoint is in two parts:

(*a*) Is it imitative?

e.g.

Bach: French Suite No. 4 in E♭ (1722–5)

E♭:

(*b*) Is it a melody line with an independent bass part?

e.g.

Bach: French Suite No. 6 in E (1722–5)

E:

If it is in three parts:

(*a*) Is it imitative in two parts, with one free part, or imitative in all three parts? If either is the case, the imitating voice will enter usually at the 5th, the 8ve, or the 4th.[2] There may be further points of imitation in the course of the piece.

e.g.

Bach: Concerto in D minor for Two Violins (*c.*1721)

[2](The study of fugue itself on which this principle is based is beyond the scope of this book; however, these exercises will give a grounding in contrapuntal techniques used in fugal writing.)

(*b*) Is it only loosely contrapuntal, with the working of figurations? This type of counterpoint may be dominated by the top part:

e.g.
Bach: French Suite No. 3 in B minor (1722–5)

Whatever type of counterpoint is involved *it will be harmonically based*, and therefore the chords and modulations should be worked out first. (This should be done even when the bass is figured.) Often, the more complicated the figuration appears, the simpler is the harmonic framework; for example, the figuration in the extract below can be harmonized with just a few chords.

Bach: French Suite No. 5 in G (1722–5)

2. *In what form is the piece?* If it is in simple binary form, for example, it is likely that the opening and closing bars of each section will be the same material. (Whatever the form, it is helpful to work out the cadence bars at the beginning, remembering that Baroque cadences frequently follow characteristic formulae.)

3. *What figuration is used?* Composers are generally economical with their material, so use the ideas already presented rather than invent new ones. If, for example, a flowing bass with suspensions above it is featured, or the part-writing is in 3rds (as in music by Corelli and Purcell), this texture should be maintained.

4. *Are there any sequences?* They are a common feature of this style and should be noted, and treated as such, in all parts. The progression of 5ths often features in sequences.[3]

FIGURATION

A study of Baroque figuration reveals a musical language in which dissonance plays an intrinsic part governed by (*a*) the strong functional progression of the harmony, and (*b*) the need to preserve the movement once set in motion. In the following

[3] See p. 47

example the harmonic progression ii–V–I–IV overrides any incidental dissonances:

Handel: Concerto Grosso Op. 6 No. 10 (1739)

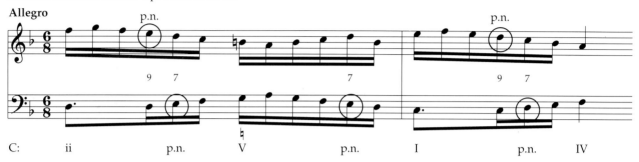

Dissonances in figuration may include suspensions (see p. 11, 70), unaccented passing notes (see p. 6), accented passing notes (see p. 16, 74), auxiliary notes (see p. 7), appoggiaturas (see p. 75), cambiata notes (see p. 18), 'echappée' notes, and anticipation notes (see p. 117 and 19). These may be found in conjunction with harmony notes, often in arpeggio figures, and 8ve leaps, especially in the bass. They are indicated here by the following abbreviations:

p.n.= passing note   d =unprepared dissonance
a.p.n.= accented passing note   app. = appoggiatura
c='cambiata' figure   e='echappée' note
s=suspension   a=anticipation note
aux.=auxiliary note (accented)

Consider the following passage, where the drive towards the cadence is aided by a variety of dissonant 'pulls'.

Bach: French Suite No. 2 in C minor (1722–5)

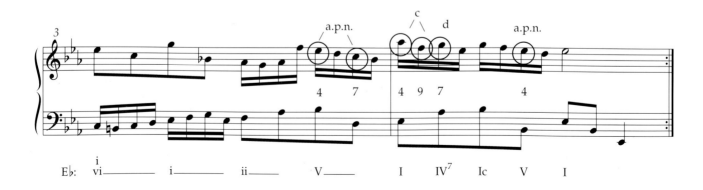

Suspensions may be decorated before they resolve;* Italian composers for the violin, notably Corelli and Vivaldi, delighted in leaps across the strings, which often involved jumps onto dissonances.

Bach: French Suite No. 2 in C minor (1722–5)

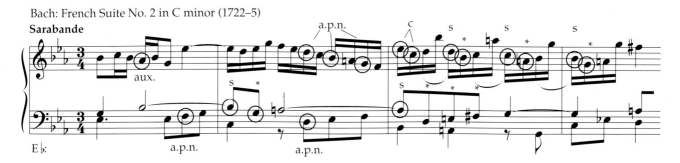

Vivaldi: Violin Concerto Op. 3 No. 6 (1712)

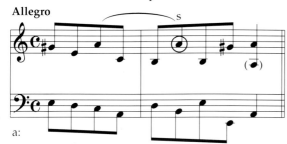

'Echappée' notes involve upward movement by step *away* from the harmony note, followed by a jump down, usually of a 3rd:

Purcell: *Dido and Aeneas* (1689)   Stanley: Organ Voluntary Vol. 1 No. 1 (1748)

The following cadential formulae should be memorized, since they are so common.

Stanley: Organ Voluntary Vol. 2 No. 1 (1752)   Greene: Air (1733)

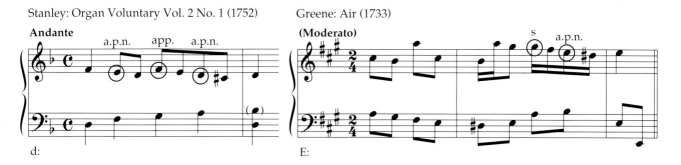

Exercise

193   Ring and identify dissonances in the figuration in these bars from Bach's *Italian Concerto* (1735).

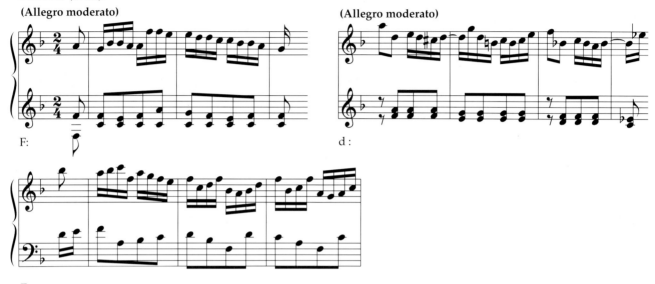

Two-part Writing

Exercises

Complete these keyboard pieces in two parts.

194   Bach: *Little Notebook for Anna Magdalena* (1722–5)

195 Ibid.

196 Bach: *Six Little Preludes* (c.1720)

197 Bach: French Suite No. 6 in E (1722–5)

198 Bach: French Suite No. 2 in C minor (1722–5)

199 Ibid.

200 Handel: Suite No. 8 for Keyboard (*c.*1733)

Instrumental and Vocal Melodies

In music consisting of an instrumental or vocal melody and a bass part, the continuo player is required to fill in the harmonies in performance. Often the bass is so strong, however, that the harmony is understood and completed by the ear.

Exercises

Complete the following extracts in two parts.

201 Lully: *Le Bourgeois Gentilhomme* (1670)

202 Handel: *Water Music* No. 8 (1717)

203 Ibid. No. 7

204 Handel: Concerto Grosso Op. 6 No. 4 (1739)

205   Handel: Concerto Grosso Op. 6 No. 8 (1739)

206   Telemann: Suite in A minor for Flute and Strings (*c.*1725)

207   Bach: Cantata No. 140 (1731)

Three-part Writing

The following example of three-part keyboard writing is taken from the chorale fugue on 'Vom Himmel hoch' in the *Weimar Tablature Book* (1704), attributed to Pachelbel. Note that the rhythm ♩♪♪ is often answered by 𝄾♪♪♪. Notice the use of imitation, suspensions and cadential patterns in this style.

'Vom Himmel hoch'

Exercises

Complete these chorale fugues from the *Weimar Tablature Book* in the same style.

208 'Herr Christ der einig Gottes Sohn'

209 'O Mensch bewein dein Sünde gross'

F:

210 'Nun komm, der Heiden Heiland'

a:

211 'Kommt hier zu mir'

g: *

* Modal key signature.

212   'Aus tiefer Not'

G:

Complete these keyboard pieces.

213   Bach: *Nine Little Preludes*, No. 6 (1720–1)

214   Bach: *Five Little Preludes*, No. 3 (*c.*1720)

c:

215   Bach: English Suite No. 5 in E minor (*c.*1715)

e:

216   Bach: English Suite No. 6 in D minor (*c.*1715)

d:

Complete in three parts these excerpts from (trio) sonatas for two violins and
continuo by Purcell (1659–95).

217 *Ten Sonatas of Four Parts*, No. 9 (*c.*1680)

218 Ibid.

219 *Twelve Sonatas of Three Parts*, No. 2 (c.1683)

220 Ibid.

Complete these excerpts from trio sonatas by Corelli (1653–1713).

221 *Sonata da Chiesa* Op. 3 No. 1 (1689)

222 Ibid.

F:

223   *Sonata da Camera* Op. 4 No. 3 (1694)

224 *Sonata da Chiesa* Op. 3 No. 4 (1689)

Complete in three parts these excerpts from works by Handel.

225 *Water Music*, No. 17 (1717)

226 *Water Music*, No. 18 (1717)

227 Concerto Grosso Op. 6 No. 5 (1739)

228 Concerto Grosso Op. 6 No. 12 (1739)

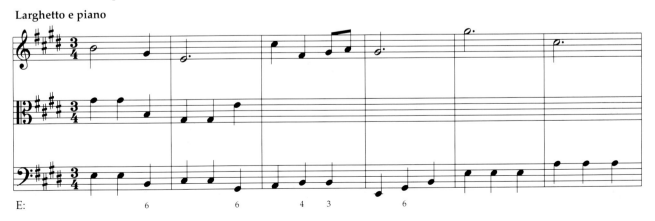

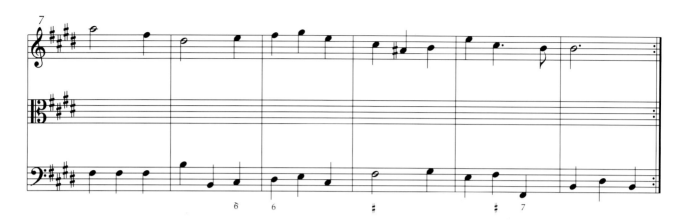

5. *The Classical Period*
(c.1740–1815)

Whereas in the 18th century music had been predominantly vocal and Italian, by 1800 it had become instrumental and German. Opera, a Baroque invention, undoubtedly continued to flourish; in the hands of Gluck, Italian, French, and German styles were merged, and Mozart's genius went on to produce masterpieces in that idiom. However, in the realm of instrumental music, the Classical period saw the establishment of the sonata principle and the development of three genres that were to dominate compositional thought for the next 150 years or so, namely the symphony, string quartet, and concerto.

The orchestra emerged as a balanced entity, with the continuo gradually discarded. Centres like Mannheim helped to establish the taste for orchestral music that was new and exciting, written by a group of 'modern' composers such as J. Stamitz (1717–57), G. C. Wagenseil (1715–77), M. G. Monn (1717–50), and two of J. S. Bach's sons, C. P. E. Bach (1714–88) and J. C. Bach (1735–82).

An entry by J. G. Sulzer in the encyclopaedia *Allgemeine Theorie der schönen Künste* (General Theory of Fine Arts) of 1771–4, describes the early Classical symphony:

The chamber symphony, which consists of an independent whole that does not lead on to anything else, is realised through a full-toned, brilliant, fiery style. The allegros of the best chamber symphonies contain large, bold thoughts, free handling of the texture, apparent disorder in melody and harmony, strongly marked rhythms of various kinds, powerful bass melodies and 'unison', 'concertante' inner parts, free imitation, often a theme treated in fugal style, abrupt transitions and aberrations from one key to another, which are the more striking the weaker the connection: strong contrasts of forte and piano, and especially the crescendo, which when combined with a rising, expressive melody has the greatest effect.

It is clear that this form now stood by itself, and was no longer an overture or introduction to a larger work. Sulzer's comments reveal the new element of contrast within a movement, where constant changes of mood produced a succession of varying musical ideas. This is an approach radically different from the late Baroque style, where a single mood or 'affection' would govern a complete movement.

After 1750 composers sought to develop a more varied and flexible style free from the 'mechanical' idioms of the past, one which would employ a greater variety of rhythms, figures, and themes. While the harmonic vocabulary used by Haydn was much the same as that of Vivaldi, the difference lay in the *way* in which it was used. Harmonic progressions were again simplified and greater emphasis placed on primary triads and their relationship to the tonal centre; as movements became longer the rate of harmonic change was slowed down. Much of the music reflected a charm, dignity, and restraint befitting its aristocratic patrons where no one, including the composer, stepped out of place. But a release of emotional expression came with the explosive statements of Beethoven, a figure who belonged appropriately to a post-revolutionary age.

The Musical Language of the Classical Period

1. STYLISTIC FEATURES DERIVED FROM BAROQUE MUSIC

Many features of the Classical style had appeared earlier in Baroque music. These include the following:

(a) The dance

Although the 18th-century suite was superseded by larger forms, many dance forms were retained, in particular the minuet, which found a place in the new symphony, sonata, and string quartet (see example (*a*) below). Moreover the character of individual dances is evident in much music, although the titles may not appear. The gigue was a favourite for last movements, as illustrated in example (*b*) below.

(*a*) Haydn: Symphony No. 95 in C minor (1791)   (*b*) Haydn: String Quartet Op. 33 No. 2 (1781)

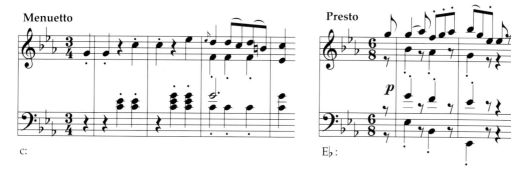

(b) The 'brilliant' style

Baroque composers, including Corelli and Vivaldi, developed the 'brilliant' style, often using sequential passages of fast figuration for a virtuoso or emotional effect. This exciting writing is very common in both the instrumental and vocal writing of Haydn and Mozart:

Mozart: 'Domine Deus' from Mass in C minor (1783)

(c) The 'learned' or strict style

The 'learned' or strict style, which included all types of contrapuntal writing, especially fugue, was now associated in particular with church music. Some composers also used the style in chamber music. The three fugal finales from Haydn's string quartets Op. 20 (1772) are powerful examples:

Haydn: String Quartet Op. 20 No. 5 (1772)

The counterpoint of Bach and Handel had a particular influence on the later works of Haydn, Mozart and Beethoven (see p. 149).

(d) The French overture style

The French overture, the creation of Lully for the court of Louis XIV, began with a slow, stately adagio, featuring dotted rhythms. This ceremonial style became an important element in Baroque music all over Europe, and was often used in the later Classical period. See, for example, the 'Rex Tremendae' from Mozart's *Requiem* (below), or the opening of his Symphony No. 39 in E♭, K. 543.

Mozart: *Requiem* (1791)

2. THE NEW FEATURES OF CLASSICAL STYLE

The new elements that were to make up the Classical style began to evolve around the 1730s, producing a simple idiom now known as the early Classical style or 'style galant'. Some of its traits remained throughout the Classical period, others were modified. The principal feature was the 'revival' of melody, which had tended to be lost in the complex textures of the high Baroque. Simple basses and accompaniments were used, and counterpoint was virtually eliminated.

J. C. Bach: Quintet in D, Op. 22 (1785)

(a) The 'singing style'

Classical melody inherited many Baroque traits, such as the use of figuration and ornamentation, as well as the forms of the recitative and aria. The influence of Italian opera was all-pervasive. Most of Mozart's music seems to be vocally conceived, for many of his instrumental melodies step straight out of the world of opera — echoing the stately utterances of the Countess[1] and Donna Anna[2] or the unsophisticated ditties of the peasant-like Papageno[3] and Zerlina[4].

Compare these examples of the 'singing style'.

Mozart: *The Marriage of Figaro* (1786)

[1] *The Marriage of Figaro* (1786).   [2] *Don Giovanni* (1787).
[3] *The Magic Flute* (1791).   [4] *Don Giovanni* (1787).

Mozart: Clarinet Quintet in A, K. 581 (1789)

The weak or 'feminine' ending phrase, together with its implication of the harmonies $\frac{6}{4}-\frac{5}{3}$, is a prevailing characteristic of the melodic line, possibly because of its long-standing association with the Italian language, in which many words have weak-ending syllables:

Beethoven: Piano Concerto No. 3 (?1800) (outline)

(b) Thematic Material

For a while, early Classical movements were often monothematic, i.e. built around a principle musical idea, a 'germ' theme, that formed the backbone of the movement. The fast movements of the 'Sturm und Drang' symphonies of Haydn are usually dominated by one or two complimentary themes, frequently announced as a unison 'gesture' or 'call to attention.'

Haydn: Symphony No. 44 ('Trauer'), (c.1771)

As the period progressed, and movements became longer, this unity was gradually superseded by greater contrasts between musical phrases, a feature of later (Classical) style in general and of Sonata form in particular.

Mozart: Symphony No. 41 in C ('Jupiter') (1788)

Another common feature was the 'Mannheim rocket' (a rising arpeggio or scale motif) which was one of the techniques used by the Mannheim composers in the mid-18th century to display the virtuosity of their famous orchestra:

K. Stamitz: Quartetto Concertante in G (?1774)

(c) Accompaniment

The use of repeated notes in the accompaniment is common. They may appear as pedal notes, which establish the key by reiterating either the tonic or dominant; this device is often called the 'Trommelbasse':

J. C. Bach: Quintet in D, Op. 22 (1785)

The tonic 'Trommelbasse' often involved the use of IVc as an auxiliary chord of I:

K. Stamitz: Violin Concerto in G (outline) (*c*.1774)

The repeated notes may engender a sense of excitement and expectancy in the music, as in the following example:

Mozart: String Quartet in C ('Dissonance'), K. 465 (1785)

Alternatively the restless quavers may be the language of despair, as in this extract from Mozart's String Quintet in G minor, K. 516 (1787):

The 'Alberti bass', a broken-chord accompaniment figure, is a common feature associated particularly with keyboard writing:

Mozart: Piano Sonata in F, K. 280 (1775)

Exercise

229 Identify the following traits of style in this extract from Mozart's Piano Sonata in C minor, K. 457 (1784). Note the succcssion of contrasting musical ideas, a feature of late Classical style:

    (a) a melody with an Alberti bass accompaniment,

    (b) a unison 'call to attention',

    (c) weak-ending phrases ('feminine endings'),

    (d) ascending arpeggio motifs,

    (e) a 'Trommelbasse' passage,

    (f) slow harmonic rhythm.

3. EXTRA-MUSICAL ASSOCIATIONS

Some writing in the Classical style has extra-musical associations. Among them are
the following:

(a) The 'military' style

The 18th century saw many battles. The march was a ceremonial representation of
war and enjoyed great popularity. There is a suggestion of the *Marseillaise* in
Mozart's Piano Concerto No. 25 in C:

Mozart: Piano Concerto No. 25 in C, K. 503 (1786)

(b) The 'Turkish' style

War with the Turks introduced their 'janissary' (military) music to Western ears; it included bass drum, triangle, and cymbals. The style can be heard in a more refined context in Mozart's opera *Il Seraglio* (1782).

(c) The hunt and the stage-coach

The hunt, the popular pastime of the upper class, had its accompanying music in the form of horn-calls, while the post-horn's signals were familiar to all travellers. There are many allusions to both in music of this period:

Mozart: Piano Sonata in F, K. 332 (1781–3)

Beethoven: Piano Sonata
Les Adieux, Op.81a (c.1810)

(d) Word-painting and programme music

Pictorial writing was particularly important in the field of opera and oratorio, where dramatic situations called for appropriate illustration. In Mozart's *Don Giovanni* (1787), for example, the fires of hell and attendant terrors are chillingly suggested in the music itself. In his oratorio *The Creation* (1798), Haydn delights in an abundance of pictorial touches:

Haydn: *The Creation* (1798)

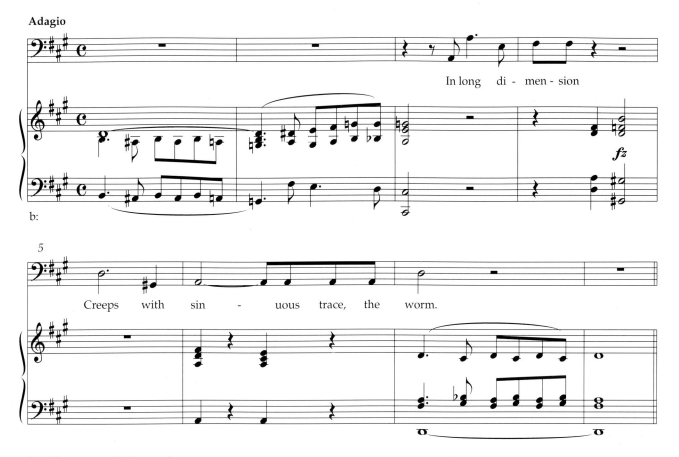

(e) 'Sturm und Drang'

By the later 18th century, the elegant superficiality of 'galant' music had given way to a more intense style. The most extreme manifestation of this was the 'Sturm und Drang' (Storm and Stress) music of the 1770s, so called after a movement in German literature,[5] which threatened to break the accepted conventions of artistic expression of the time. It sought to convey passionate feeling by the use of minor keys, chromaticism, and dissonance in movements of rhythmic drive and intensity; see, for example, Gluck's 'Dance of the Furies' from 'Orfeo' (1762), Haydn's Symphonies No. 44 in E minor ('Trauer'), No. 45 in F♯ minor ('Farewell'), and No. 49 in F minor ('La Passione'), and Mozart's Symphony No. 25 in G minor.

Along similar lines, C. P. E. Bach's keyboard style, with its swift changes of mood, fantasia-like elaboration, and dissonant harmonies, all expressive of intense feeling, was summed up by his contemporaries in the word *Empfindsamkeit,* or 'sensibility'. Later Classical music was characterized by these swift changes of mood.

4. THE BAROQUE 'INFLUENCE'

In the early 1780s Baron van Swieten introduced Haydn and Mozart to the music of Bach and Handel. The effect on both composers was profound and was evident in

---

[5] *Sturm und Drang* is the name of a drama by Klinger (1776) which anticipates some of the ideas of Romanticism. These are also present in Goethe's *Werther* (1774).

their own music after that date. *The Creation* and the late string quartets of Haydn, the *Requiem* and the last symphonies and string quintets of Mozart are works reflecting a new seriousness and intensity, only made possible by the use of the contrapuntal techniques of the Baroque. The closing section of Mozart's last symphony, No. 41 ('Jupiter') is a powerful example. Beethoven, who played Bach's '48' (Preludes and Fugues) and who worshipped Handel, took contrapuntal writing into new worlds of musical experience with his fugues, for piano in the sonatas Op. 101, 106, and 110, and for string quartet, notably the 'Grosse Fuge', Op. 133.

Beethoven: Quartet in C♯ minor, Op. 131 (1826)

Adagio ma non troppo e molto espress.

Aspects of the Harmonic Language of the Classical Period

1. PRINCIPAL FEATURES

Often the harmony of Classical music is surprisingly simple, with a predominance of primary triads and their inversions; of particular importance is the 7th of the dominant 7th chord, which may now function in the chord and in the melody line without preparation. Several harmonic formulae, including the passing and cadential $^6_4$ and various cadence patterns, are common. These will be examined in the following pages.

Exercises

Work these examples, using primary triads where possible.

230 Beethoven: Symphony No. 5 in C minor (1807–8)

231 Haydn: *The Creation* (1798)

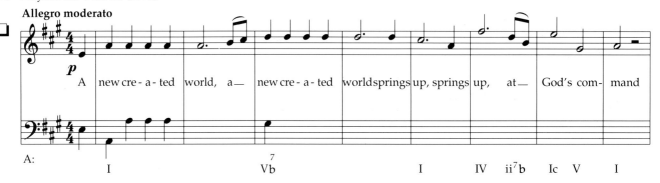

As movements became longer, harmonic rhythm (the rate of chord change) tended
to slow down, but it quickened at the cadence bars.

Exercises

Listen to these examples and label the chords.

232   Haydn: String Quartet in D, Op. 76 No. 5 (1797)

233   Mozart: Symphony No. 40 in G minor (1788)

234   Complete this extract from Mozart's *Eine kleine Nachtmusik* K. 525 (1787).

(a) The use of the dominant 7th

The dominant 7th chord, with its unique ability to define key and to 'clinch' a modulation, is very important in music of the tonal period. It no longer requires preparation and is found in every inversion including the 2nd. Its qualities as an expressive chord are sometimes overlooked, but notice its effect before chord vi in the two following examples; the 7th makes *all* the difference:

Mozart: Clarinet Quintet in A, K. 581 (1789)

Mozart: *The Magic Flute* (1791)

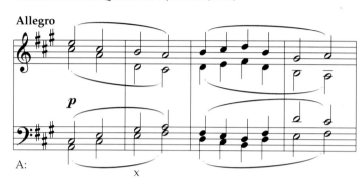

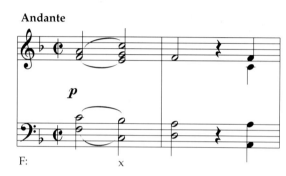

Exercises

Listen to these extracts and identify V⁷ chords and inversions.

235 Beethoven: Piano Sonata in C minor, Op. 13 (1798)

236 Beethoven: Violin Sonata in A, Op. 47 (1803)

Harmonize the following passages, using V⁷ at x. Listen carefully to each extract to identify the inversions used.

237 Mozart: *The Magic Flute* (1791)

238 Mozart: *Don Giovanni* (1787)

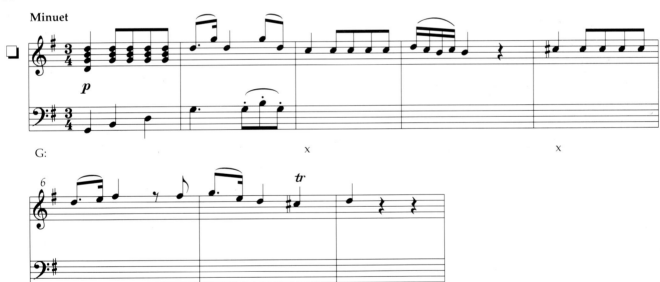

239 Beethoven: Piano Concerto No. 4 in G (1805–6)

Andante con moto, molto cantabile

e:

(b) Chords of the 9th, 11th and 13th

Thirds may be added to a triad, usually the dominant, to make these chords. Although chords of the 9th and 13th can be seen as the result of part-writing, i.e. the movement of suspensions, appoggiaturas, or accented passing notes, by the mid-18th century their sound was so characteristic that they may be thought of as chords in their own right in music of this period. As free-standing chords they belong mainly to the late 18th and 19th centuries.

F: V⁷   V⁹ (major)   V⁹ (minor)   V¹¹   V¹³ (major)   V¹³ (minor)

It is helpful to remember that:
  (i) a convincing 9th chord usually requires the presence of the 7th;
  (ii) a convincing 11th chord usually requires the presence of the 9th;
  (iii) a convincing 13th chord usually requires the presence of the 7th, 9th or 11th.

Schubert: *Atzenbrucker Deutsche*, No. 3 (c.1815)   Schubert: *Valses nobles*, Op. 77 (c.1826)

b: C:

V⁹(minor)   ib   V⁹(major)

The *Dominant minor 9th* chord, with its dominant root, is stronger than the diminished 7th, retaining the latter's quality of pathos, as the examples opposite show.

Exercises

Identify the minor 9th chords.

240 Mozart: String Quintet in G minor, K. 516 (1787)

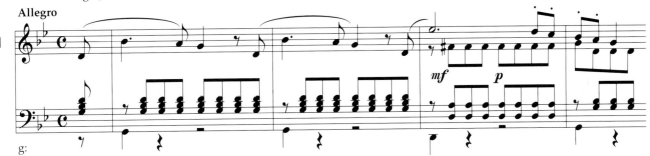

241 Mozart: *The Magic Flute* (1791)

Chords of the 11th are rare.

The *dominant 13th* chord is akin to III⁺b but includes the 7th, which adds to its poignancy in the minor key:

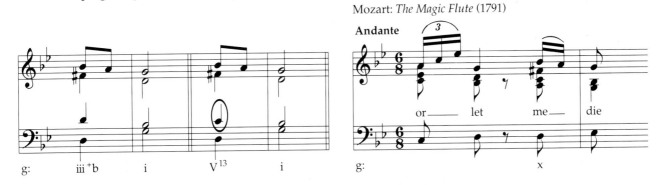

Mozart: *The Magic Flute* (1791)

(c) The diminished 7th chord

As described in Chapter 2, the diminished 7th frequently functions as a dominant substitute (vii^d7) in the minor key for expressive purposes.

In the following example the diminished 7th appears in a modulating sequence; see also the example on p. 166.

Schubert: Agnus Dei from Mass in G (1815)

e: a:x   g:x   e:x

Any note of the diminished 7th chord may appear in the bass.

Exercise

Indicate the diminished 7th chords in the following extract. Notice how the augmented chords also increase the tension of this passage.

242   Mozart: opening of the *Requiem* (1791)

(d) The use of the passing $\frac{6}{4}$ and $\frac{6}{3}$
   (3)

Both the $\frac{6}{4}$ and the $\frac{6}{3}$ are commonly used as passing chords and create smooth part-movement:
   (3)

Haydn: 'Nelson' Mass (1798)

Exercises using the passing $\frac{6}{4}$ and $\frac{6}{3}$ may be found on p. 158.
   (3)

2. THE HARMONY AT THE CADENCE

(a) Repetition of tonic and dominant chords

The assertion of tonality, which at times seems obsessive, is an integral part of the harmonic thinking in this period, almost its *raison d'être*! It is summed up in the principle of sonata form, in which the case for tonality is argued in countless eloquent examples. In very simple terms the sonata principle may be thought of as an outward journey *away* from the 'home' key and a return journey *back* to 'home'. Beethoven, in his 5th Symphony, allows himself 40 bars of cadence chords at the end of his return journey, after which there is no doubt at all that 'home' is C major.

Exercise

Label the chords in this extract.

243 Mozart: Overture to *The Magic Flute* (1791)

(b) The cadential $\frac{6}{4}$

This may feature as part of a perfect cadence (Ic–V–I) or an imperfect cadence (Ic–V) and is to be thought of as a decoration of the dominant chord. (In the Baroque period the less 'comfortable' 4–3 suspension was more often used.) It is frequently preceded by iib. The progression is sometimes decorated, and in keyboard music especially this may take the form of a trill:

Mozart: Piano Sonata in D, K. 284 (1775)

Exercises

Complete these passages, using the cadential and passing $\frac{6}{4}$ and $\frac{6}{3}$ where possible.

244   Haydn: *The Creation* (1798)

245   Mozart: *The Marriage of Figaro* (1786)

246   Haydn: 'Nelson' Mass (1798)

Glo-ri-a in ex - cel - sis De-o,   Glo-ri-a, glo-ri-a   in ex-cel -sis, in ex - cel - sis De - o.

247 Beethoven: Symphony No. 9 (1822–4)

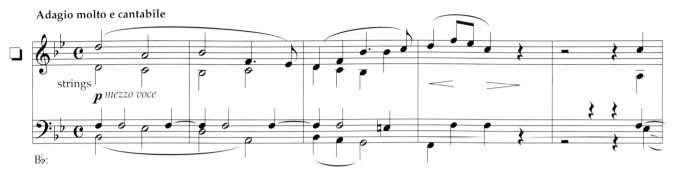

(c) The retardation at the cadence

This is another example of the weak-ending cadence, like the cadential $^6_4$. It usually takes the form of an upward-moving double or triple suspension and often follows the cadential $^6_4$.

Exercises

Label the chords at the cadence.

248 Mozart: *The Magic Flute* (1791)

Take down the bass and complete the harmonization of this passage.

249   Mozart: Clarinet Trio K. 498 (1786)

(d) The interrupted cadence and cadential extension

The interrupted cadence is always a musical 'surprise', however slight, and usually results in some form of cadential extension in order to reach the tonic chord:

Mozart: *The Magic Flute* (1791)

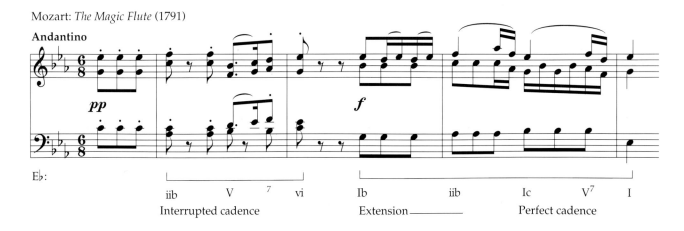

Exercise

Complete the harmonization of this passage by Beethoven.

250   Beethoven: Piano Concerto No. 5, 'Emperor' (1809)

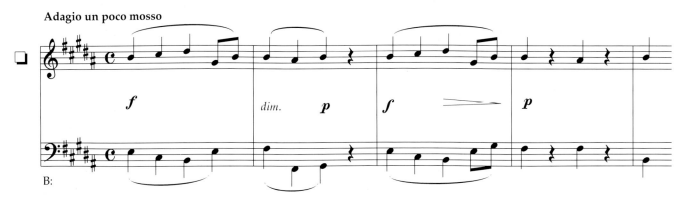

For a further example of the interrupted cadence, see p. 163.

(e) Frequent harmonic formulae at the cadence

The most common formula is the sequence of chords at the end of the progression
of 5ths, i.e. vi–ii–(Ic)–V–I.

Exercises

Take down this example:

251   Beethoven: Symphony No. 6 (1808)

Complete the harmonization of this passage, noting the cadence progressions.

252   Mozart: Piano Concerto No. 17 in G, K. 453 (1784)

Fill in the chords in this passage, noting the progression of 5ths (bars 4–8) and the horn 5th (bars 1–2).

253   Beethoven: Violin Concerto in D (1806)

(f) The use of 'coloured' chords at the cadence

The 'coloured' chords used in this context include the Neapolitan 6th, the diminished 7th, and the augmented 6th.

   (i) *The Neapolitan 6th chord.*[6] This is a major chord, usually in a minor key, built on the flattened supertonic. Up to the end of the Classical era it was invariably found in its 1st inversion, appearing in root position in the 19th century. Since it commonly resolves to ic-V (as in the example opposite) it can be seen to function in the same way as a diatonic iib. The chord has an expressive role and is often dwelt upon, emphasizing the juxtaposition of major with minor:

[6] See p. 63

Mozart: Piano Concerto No. 23 in A, K. 488 (1786)

(ii) *The diminished 7th chord.*[7] The diminished 7th chord may function at a cadence as either a dominant (vii^{d7}) or a secondary dominant ($\sharp$iv^{d7} or $\sharp$i^{d7}). As a diminished 7th of the dominant key, it can add both drama and pathos to music in a minor key: see for example the thrilling interrupted cadence at the closing bars of the Kyrie of Mozart's *Requiem* (1791):

[7] See pp. 61 and 155

Exercise

254 Take down the bass and label the chords in this passage from Mozart's opera *The Magic Flute* (1791). Note again the role of the diminished 7th in this cadential extension.

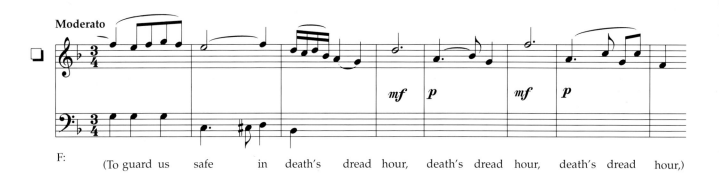

F:

(To guard us safe in death's dread hour, death's dread hour, death's dread hour,)

(iii) *The augmented 6th chord*. For reasons unknown there are three varieties of augmented 6th chord: Italian, German, and French. Each is usually built on the minor 6th of the key, with the augmented 6th sounding above it. The Italian and German sixths are derived from chord iv⁷, and the French from chord II⁷; the chromatic alterations create strong movement to the dominant, often via Ic. The figurings in the examples below give a clear idea of the other intervals involved. It will be observed that the Italian and German augmented 6th chords sound in isolation like a dominant 7th, whereas their French counterpart has a nebulous quality, beloved of Romantic composers.

C/c: IVb(altered) V   ♯6 Aug.6th (It.) V   ♯6 Aug.6th (Ger.) (ic) V   ♯6 Aug.6th (Fr.) V
                                3   5   4
                                                           3   3

Exercises

255 Write augmented 6th chords and their resolutions in the keys of C minor, G major, A major, and D minor.

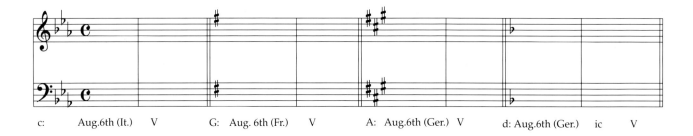

c: Aug.6th (It.)   V   G: Aug. 6th (Fr.)   V   A: Aug.6th (Ger.) V   d: Aug.6th (Ger.)   ic   V

Identify the augmented 6th chord in the following two extracts.

256 Haydn: String Quartet in D, Op. 76 No. 5 (1797)   **257** Beethoven: Piano Sonata *Les Adieux*, Op. 81a (c.1810)

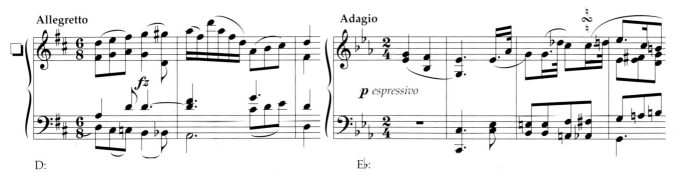

D: E♭:

Listen to the following passages and fill in the harmony at x.

258 Schubert: Symphony No. 9 in C (1828)   **259** Beethoven: Piano Sonata in C♯ minor, Op. 27 No. 2 (1801)

a: x   x   x   c♯:   x   x

260 Mozart: Clarinet Quintet in A, K. 581 (1789)

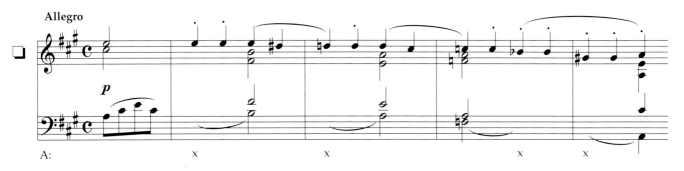

A: x   x   x   x

261 Mozart: Divertimento for String Trio in E♭, K. 563 (1788)

e♭:   f: X

3. CHROMATIC MOVEMENT AND DISSONANCE

(a) Chromaticism

As has already been suggested, chromaticism in music is frequently associated with grief, despair, and anguish, from Dowland and Monteverdi through to Wagner and Strauss. This passage from Mozart's opera *The Magic Flute* (1791), with its descending chromatic bass, is imbued with agitation and despair, reflecting Pamina's state of mind as she determines to kill herself:

Haydn saw chromaticism as the breakdown of harmonic 'law and order', hence its use in the 'Representation of Chaos' (the prelude to *The Creation*, 1798):

In the same work, 'light' is represented simply by C major, brilliantly scored.

(b) The suspension [8]

The suspension may be used to 'move' music forward, as in the effective passage below from *The Creation*, depicting the rising sun.

[8] See pp. 11, 70, 98 and 117.

Exercise

262 Identify the suspensions used and discuss their effect in this passage.

D:

Note, in another mood, this passage from the opening of Mozart's *Requiem* (1791), where the dissonances sharpen the numb despair, expressed in the weary tread of the bass:

d:

(c) The appoggiatura and accented passing note [9]

These dissonances occur in both fast and slow music as a characteristic decoration of the melodic line in music of this period. Notice their use in the aria quoted below from Mozart's *The Magic Flute*, where Pamina laments her lost love and sees death as the only release from her suffering.

Exercises

Ring the appoggiaturas and accented passing notes in the following passages.

263 Mozart: *The Magic Flute* (1791)

g:

[9] See pp. 16, 74–5 and 100.

264 Haydn: Symphony No. 88 in G (?1787)

265 Beethoven: Symphony No. 3 in E♭, 'Eroica' (1803)

The use of the appoggiatura as an unprepared dissonance increased during this period, and became a prominent feature of 19th-century Romantic harmony. Consider the passionate opening of the last movement of Beethoven's String Quartet in A minor, Op. 132 (1825), where an appoggiatura marks the climax of the soaring melody:

Exercise

266   Listen to the opening bars of the 'Lacrymosa' from Mozart's *Requiem* (1791). How
effective is the word-setting? Consider the following in your discussion:
  (*a*) the melodic line;
  (*b*) the accompaniment figures;
  (*c*) the use of rests;
  (*d*) the harmonic language: chromatic writing, dissonance, coloured chords,
       etc.

Mozart: 'Lacrymosa', *Requiem* (1791)

(Ah! that day of tears and mourning! From the dust of earth returning, man for judgement
must prepare him!)

6. Classical Style: The String Quartet

'Chamber music' in the 18th century referred to music performed in the small concert-rooms and salons of the aristocracy. The term embraced a large number of assorted forms, including the concerto, symphony, sonata, divertimento, and serenade, played by many combinations of instruments. In the latter part of the century the term 'chamber style' referred specifically to music with one instrument to a part, associated with intimate domestic music-making.

As the number of competent amateurs increased, so did the demand for chamber music. That the string quartet was a popular ensemble is evident from many contemporary writings: 'this instrumental composition for four instruments, which has been such a favourite for many years, is a special category of sonata, and in the strict sense, consists of four concerting instruments, none of which can claim exclusively the role of a leading voice.' (H. Koch, *Musikalisches Lexikon*, 1802.)

Origins

The string quartet developed from the Baroque trio sonata, which was usually scored for two violins (or flutes), viola da gamba, and continuo, a three-part texture with the keyboard filling in the harmonies. The string quartet emerged in the 1750s, as a light, serenade-like piece in which the number of movements varied from two to seven; it was probably played out of doors in the streets and courtyards of Vienna, hence the absence of the keyboard. Haydn gave the name 'divertimenti a quattro' to his string quartets up to Op. 20 (1772).

The Character of the Writing

These early quartets were generally dominated by the 1st violin; later quartets still gave the leader the most prominent part. The other parts played an accompanying role, the addition of the viola providing a 'tenor' voice to fill out the gap left in the middle by the lack of keyboard realization.

Accompaniment figures were many and varied, including arpeggio and broken-chord figurations, repeated notes, pizzicato patterns, and held chords, or a combination of these. Movement in 3rds (l0ths) and 6ths was a common feature:

Haydn: String Quartet in G, Op. 9 No. 3 (c.1769)

Frequently the texture would fall into two parts, the violins 1 and 2 together, an 8ve apart, and the viola and cello together, also an 8ve apart. Canonic writing was sometimes used, as in the following extract from Haydn's 'Witches' Minuet':

Haydn: String Quartet in D minor, Op. 76 No. 2 (?1797)

The melody line was often doubled at the 8ve:

Mozart: String Quartet in E♭, K. 428 (1783)

E♭:

Unison passages were common, usually at the beginning or at the cadence bars:

Haydn: String Quartet in C, Op. 9 No. 1 (*c.*1769)

C:

Contrapuntal passages involving imitation were often used. Fugues and fugal textures, as found in the Baroque *sonata da chiesa* (church sonata), were a regular feature, e.g. in the last movements of Haydn's Op. 20 Nos. 2, 5, and 6:

Haydn: String Quartet in F minor, Op. 20 No. 5 (1772)

f:

The development of the form showed the gradual liberation of the 2nd violin, viola, and cello into equal and independent partners with the leader, partly through the use of contrapuntal textures. The later quartets of Haydn, the six quartets dedicated to Haydn by Mozart, and the Op. 59 and late quartets of Beethoven are all major achievements in this form:

Mozart: String Quartet in G, K. 387 (1782)

G:

The study of textures in the string quartet is fascinating. Classical composers achieved endless variety in the spacing and grouping of the four instruments, as well as in the type of music they played, homophonic or contrapuntal. An important contributory factor was the use of rests, which allowed the music to 'breathe', and pointed both the rhythm and the sonorities:

Mozart: String Quartet in D minor, K. 421 (1783)

F:

Virtuoso passages involving fast semiquaver figuration and leaps, a trait inherited from the Baroque, were a feature of the style, which also delighted in swift contrasts of mood within the movement: see, for example, the first movement of Haydn's String Quartet Op. 76 No. 4 (?1797):

g:

In a passage from the slow movement of the same work, notice the way in which Haydn varies the texture and spacing:

Some Comments on String Writing in the 18th Century

The services of any string player in the class should be called upon to demonstrate the various technical points mentioned in this section.

1. RANGE

The instruments in the string quartet, two violins, viola, and cello, are tuned as follows:

Early string quartet writing reveals a fairly conservative range for each of the instruments. The late quartets of Haydn and Mozart extend the upper ranges of the 1st violin and cello in particular.

The virtuosity encouraged by Locatelli and Vivaldi in the newly invented violin concerto demanded the use of higher positions. Leopold Mozart in his *Violinschule* (1756) wrote that positions could be put to 'elegant' use, and recommended that the chin should be used to grip the instrument to give greater security in 'shifts' (not universal practice in 1756). These 'shifts' should be made where possible on repeated notes, open strings, and dotted notes, to preserve the uniformity of tone colour of a single string.

2. TONE AND TECHNIQUE

(a) Vibrato

The use of vibrato, an effect produced by rocking movements of the finger on the string with the help of the wrist, was accepted practice in the Baroque period, especially in the performance of slow, lyrical music. Geminiani (1687–1762), a pupil of Corelli, advocated its use on short notes 'to make their sound more agreeable' (*The Art of Playing on the Violin*, 1751). Tartini (1692–1770), recognized the application of different speeds of vibrato, depending on the expression needed.

(b) Bowing

The 18th century attached much importance to the bow in achieving an expressive 'nuanced' tone. (The tension of the older bow was less than that of the modern bow, so that a *sf* stroke was hardly possible.) Leopold Mozart, who advocated a 'manly' tone, was the first to mention speed as a factor in the volume of tone. The type of bow-stroke used depended on the character and tempo of the music to be played. A down-bow was probably used for the first stressed note on a strong beat (a convention called the 'rule of down-bow'), even if two down-bows came together.

Slurring. Slurring, or the playing of two or more notes in one bow, was used to achieve 'legato'. It was indicated by slurs, or by the word 'legato' (when it applied to the whole piece). Playing in the legato style generally involved the 'nuanced' sound. This depended on the dynamic usually applied to the bow-stroke, a *crescendo*, or a *diminuendo*, or a *messa di voce* ($<\ >$), as opposed to using a 'straight' sound. Notes were rarely slurred over the barline, unless, of course, a syncopated effect was required, since this would affect the rhythmic clarity.

 = legato slurred tremolo[1]— in which the bow's impulses on the string meant that there was no actual break in the sound.

 = staccato slurred tremolo, often called 'portato'—in which the bow was stopped on the string. This was associated with andante or adagio movements in the 18th century.

Mozart: String Quartet in C, K. 465 (1785)

---

[1] 18th-century term for 'vibrato' — 'a natural quivering on the violin' (L. Mozart, 1756).

Articulation. Particular conventions were followed in articulation (the degree of separation between notes and the emphasis given to them). Notes without specific slurred or staccato markings were generally played shorter than actually written (*detaché*). Leopold Mozart listed various bow-strokes (his 'divisions'), which included *crescendo*, indicated by $<$, *diminuendo,* $>$, and *messa di voce*, shown by $<>$ on one note.

(c) Other devices

Pizzicato (or pizz.). This term is an instruction to pluck the string, generally with the right hand. Monteverdi's players had used two fingers; by 1750 only the index finger was employed.

Multiple-stops. This is a collective term for chords on the violin; e.g. double-stopping is the playing of strings simultaneously. There are many examples of this device. Three- and four-part chords were usually arpeggiated quickly, with the melody note sustained.

Other terms for string techniques, including *col legno* (on the wood of the bow), *sul ponticello* (on the bridge) and *glissando* (sliding), were known in the 17th century, but rarely used before 1800.

(d) Dynamics

These ranged from *pp* to *ff*, although often only *p* and *f* were used. Other signs include *mf, rf, sf, cresc.*, and *dim*. Beethoven used *ppp* near the end of the String Quartet Op. 59 No. 1 (1806). Composers tended to be inconsistent in the amount of dynamic instruction they gave in different works.

Exercises

Listen, if possible, to the following extracts and discuss:
(a) the bowing, dynamics, and other instructions relating to performance;
(b) the texture of the music, noting, where relevant, the effectiveness of the scoring, the spacing of the parts, the use of rests, and the accompaniment figurations.

267   Mozart: String Quartet in D, K. 575 (1789)

268   Haydn: String Quartet in C, Op. 74 No. 1 (1793)

Andantino grazioso

G:

Complete the 2nd violin and viola parts, maintaining the given textures. As you listen to each passage, notice the writing in 3rds, rests in the texture, imitative writing, and dynamics. Work out the harmony before you complete the extract.

269   Mozart: String Quartet in D minor, K. 421 (1783)

270   Ibid.

271   Mozart: String Quartet in C, K. 465 (1785)

Like that of the Baroque period, all counterpoint of the later 18th century is
harmonically based, and chords should therefore be identified before each exercise
is attempted; in most cases the more complicated the figuration, the simpler the
harmonic structure.

Work these extracts from string quartets in two parts. Remember to indicate the bowing.

272   Haydn: String Quartet in F, Op. 17 No. 2 (1771)

273   String Quartet in C, Op. 3 No. 2 (formerly attributed to Haydn)[2]

274   Haydn: String Quartet in C, Op. 9 No. 1 (*c*.1769)

[2]   Op. 3 is now believed to be by R. Hoffstetter (1742–1815). See *The Musical Times*, July 1964. Alan Tyson and H. C. Robbins Landon, 'Who composed Haydn's Op. 3?'

Complete the writing for two violins from Mozart's 12 Duos, K. 487 (1785).

275 No. 9

Menuetto

G:

276 No. 10

Andante

G:

277 No. 11

Complete the following for string quartet.

278 String Quartet in C, Op. 3 No. 2 (formerly attributed to Haydn)

279 Haydn: String Quartet in B♭, Op. 33 No. 4 (1781)

B♭:

280 Haydn: String Quartet in F minor, Op. 20 No. 5 (1772)

F:

281   Haydn: String Quartet in B♭, Op. 2 No. 6 (?c.1761)

282   String Quartet in F, Op. 3 No. 5 (formerly attributed to Haydn)

283 Ibid.

Menuetto

284 Haydn: String Quartet in C, Op. 9 No. 1 (*c.*1769)

Adagio

285 Haydn: String Quartet in C, Op. 9 No. 1 (*c.*1769)

Menuetto
Poco allegretto

286 Haydn: String Quartet in C minor, Op. 17 No. 4 (1771)

7. The Early Romantic Period
(c.1810–50)

The period *c*.1810–1914 is known in the arts as the Romantic era. Its roots can be traced back to the 18th century, to events such as the French Revolution (1789) and the publication of Goethe's *Werther* (1774), both reflecting a new spirit of individualism, the one on the political front, also realized in the far-reaching national movements, the other on the personal, realized in the preoccupation with self and the releasing of passions and emotions contained in the interests of Classical poise and elegance. The composer, starting with Beethoven, was now treated as a revered genius, rather than the servant of the aristocracy .

The aim was the fusion of the arts, summed up in Wagner's *Gesamtkunstwerk* (the 'all-embracing art-work of the future'); a composition might therefore have a 'programme', such as is found in Berlioz's 'Fantastic' Symphony. The composer was frequently a connoisseur of the arts; Schumann, Berlioz, and Wagner were important literary figures in their day; Wagner was also committed to politics and even exiled for his part in the 1848 Revolution. Romantic composers, writers, and painters were always striving for some kind of artistic Utopia, in which universal love in harmony with the natural world, the dream of Rousseau, would prevail; this idealism intensified as the Industrial Revolution, with its attendant abuses, progressed.

Yet the age was full of contradictions: an obsession with the grotesque and satanic accompanied the quest for beauty and the supernatural; the positive optimism found in the symphonic finales of Beethoven, Brahms, or Dvořák was contrasted with the introspective despair of many songs in Schubert's *Winterreise* or in the final pages of Tchaikovsky's Sixth Symphony; a conscious looking-forward to posterity went hand in hand with a nostalgia for the past. The vast assembly of voices and instruments (in, for example, Berlioz's *Requiem*), together with the passion for virtuosity in all its forms, was seen alongside the exquisite, simple miniature, a song by Schubert or a delicate mazurka by Chopin.

The artist, then, was primarily concerned with the communication of his feelings and emotions; to achieve this the musical language was extended, the forces used enlarged where necessary, and the inherited 18th-century forms adapted or, if found to be restrictive, rejected.

As the 19th century progressed, chromatic harmony became increasingly important, as for example in the works of Wagner, Wolf, and Richard Strauss; this led in the 20th century to the abandonment of tonality by some composers, and to the new school of serial writing of Schoenberg, Berg, and Webern. In another direction, Debussy and the Impressionists evolved a new language which also undermined the tonal system.

Note: A detailed study of 19th-century harmony is outside the scope of this book. What follows in this chapter is a brief resumé of various chords and progressions characteristic of this period; students may find it useful to write these out in various keys before attempting the exercises. For further information on the subject, see Robert Ottman's excellent *Advanced Harmony* (Prentice-Hall, Inc., Englewood Cliffs, New Jersey, 1961).

The Extension of the Harmonic Language, c.1810–50

In the music of this period the range of chords is consistently wider than that in earlier works. Most of the chords are already to be found in the music of Mozart and Beethoven; what is different is the frequency with which they are used. An extreme example is the chord of the diminished 7th, which, while used sparingly by Classical composers, almost suffers from over-exposure in the hands of Weber and Mendelssohn. The criticism is sometimes made that an 'overdose' of chromaticism results in sentimental or decadent music. In general, however, an intuitive sense of taste governed 19th-century composers, and their harmonic language may be seen as the expressive tool of their craft.

1. DIATONIC SECONDARY 7ths [1]

These are often found in sequence, in conjunction with the progression of 5ths.

Exercise

Label the chords in the following extract, noting the 7ths.

287   Schumann: *Dichterliebe*, No. 5 (1840)

---

[1] Students are referred to p. ix in the Introduction where the triads in a key together with their most frequent alterations, additions and labelling are set out.

song   of   this love   of   mine.

2. ALTERED CHORDS

The chromatic alteration of chords in a key was a common procedure in the 19th
century. Any chord might be treated in this way. 7ths were often added. However,
the chord will retain its diatonic function e.g. ii moving to V, whatever the alteration
and/or addition(s). See ex. 290.

Exercises

Identify the altered chords in the following passages.

288   Schubert: Symphony No. 5 (1816)

This excursion into the key of the flattened 6th, returning 'home' via the augmented
6th, is a common occurrence in Schubert's music.

289 Mendelssohn: Overture, *A Midsummer Night's Dream* (1826)

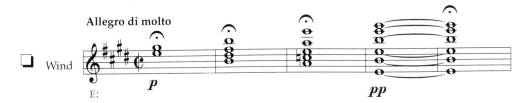

290 Schumann: *Dichterliebe*, No. 7 (1840)

I blame thee not, al-tho' my heart must break,

*(a) Altered chords as secondary dominants*²

Exercises

Complete the altered chords in these examples.

291 Schumann: *Album for the Young*, No. 43 (1848) **292** Chopin: *Ballade* Op. 47 (1841)

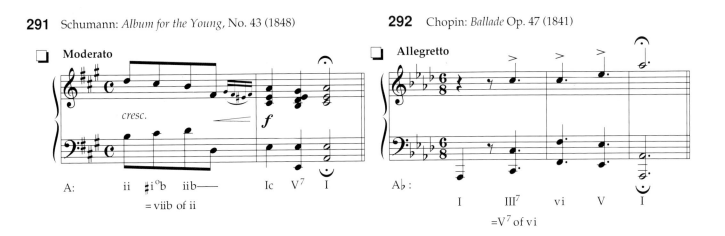

A: ii ♯iᵒb iib—— Ic V⁷ I
= viib of ii

A♭: I III⁷ vi V I
=V⁷ of vi

² See pp. 49 and 61.

(b) The augmented triad [3]

This alteration is usually applied to I, IV, and V in a major key; only III is augmented in a minor key:

Exercises

Label the chords in the following extracts, identifying the augmented triad in each.

293 Wagner: *Siegfried* (1871)

294 Wagner: *The Valkyrie* (1856) (Valkyrie motif)

---

[3] See pp. 20 and 156.

(c) The Neapolitan 6th chord (♭IIb) [4]

Exercises

Identify the Neapolitan 6th chords in the following examples.

295 Schumann: *Dichterliebe* No. 8 (1840)

'Tis she who caused my sor-row, And broke my heart in twain.

296 Wagner: *Tristan and Isolde* (1859)

Music of this period may *modulate* to the key of the Neapolitan 6th chord:

Chopin: Mazurka Op. 7 No. 2 (1830–1)

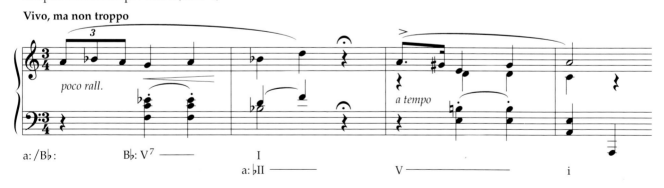

[4] See pp.63 and 162.

(d) The augmented 6th chord [5]

Exercises

Listen to these passages and complete the augmented 6th chords at x.

297   Schubert: Octet in F (1824)

298   Wagner: *Tristan and Isolde* (1859)

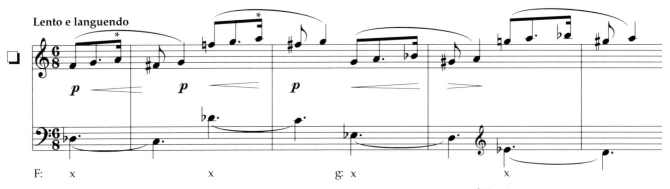

* an unusual version of the augmented 6th chord featuring an augmented 5th. $\begin{pmatrix} \sharp 6 \\ \natural 5 \\ 3 \end{pmatrix}$

[5] See p. 164.

3. CHORDS OF THE 9th, 11th, AND 13th [6]

Exercises

Identify the chords of the 9th, 11th, and 13th in the following extracts.

299   Liszt: Piano Sonata in B minor (1853)

300   Mendelssohn: Octet for Strings (1825)

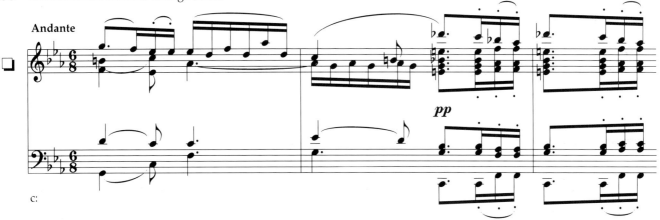

301   Mendelssohn: *Song without Words* Op. 53 No. 2 (1841)

302   Wagner: *The Rhine Gold* (1854) (sword motif)

[6] See p. 154.

4. UNPREPARED DISSONANCE: THE APPOGGIATURA [7]

While the suspension is still in frequent use, it is the unprepared dissonance, the appoggiatura, which is an especially prominent feature in music of the 19th century.

Exercises

Ring the appoggiaturas and note their effect.

303 Schumann: Piano Concerto in A minor (1845)

304 Schumann: 'Valse noble' from *Carnaval* (1835)

5. MODULATION [8]

Romantic composers explored the effects of far-reaching modulation; contrasts of key within a movement, particularly to unrelated tonal centres, are common.

Exercises

Identify the modulations in the following passages. How are the modulations effected?

305 Berlioz: *Les Nuits d'Été* (1834–41)

[7] See pp. 75 and 167.
[8] See p. 66.

306   Schubert: Quintet in C (1828)

G: V

307   Chopin: Mazurka Op. 56 No. 1 (1843)

B:

Exercises

Complete these extracts for pianoforte, keeping to the style of the opening.

308   Schubert: Ländler (?1821)

A:

309   Chopin: Nocturne Op. 62 No. 2 (1846)

310   Schubert: Impromptu Op. 142 No. 3 (1828)

311   Chopin: Mazurka in A minor, Op. 7 No. 2 (1830–1)

Exercises

Complete these extracts from 19th-century chamber and vocal works; some are aural
exercises to be worked in class.

312   Schubert: Octet in F (1824) (outline)

313 Ibid.

314 Schubert: Quartettsatz in C minor (1820)

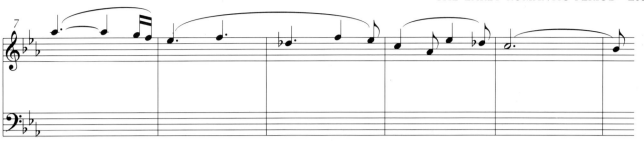

315 Schubert: Fantasia in F minor, D. 940 (1828) (outline)[9]

[9] The original is for piano duet (four hands).

Exercises

Complete these piano accompaniments to songs by Schubert and Schumann. The opening introductions each indicate the style of the writing, which should be maintained throughout the piece.

316   Schubert: 'Der Wegweiser' (The Guide Post) from *Winterreise* (1827)

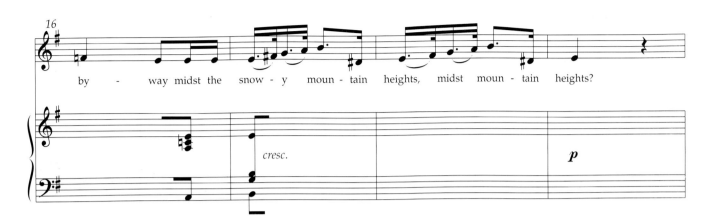

by - way midst the snow - y moun - tain heights, midst moun - tain heights?

cresc.

p

317 Schubert: 'Der Neugierige' (The Enquirer) from *Die schöne Müllerin* (1823)

318 Schubert: 'Gretchen am Spinnrade' (Gretchen at the Spinning-wheel) (1814)

Complete this extract in three parts.

319 Mendelssohn: Terzetto (The Angels) from *Elijah* (1846)

Select Bibliography

Deryck Cooke	*The Language of Music* (O.U.P., 1959)
Richard Crocker	*A History of Musical Style* (McGraw-Hill, 1966)
Richard Goldman	*Harmony in Western Music* (Barrie & Rockcliff, 1968)
Paul Hindemith	*Traditional Harmony* (Schott & Co., 1943)
The Juilliard Report	*Teaching the Literature and Materials of Music* (1953)
Ivor Keys	*The Texture of Music from Purcell to Brahms* (Dennis Dobson, 1961)
Noel Long	*Harmony and Style* (Faber & Faber, 1968)
Robert Ottman	*Advanced Harmony* (Prentice-Hall Inc. N.J., 1961)
Leonard Ratner	*Classic Music: Expression, Form and Style* (Macmillan, 1980)
Charles Rosen	*The Classical Style* (Faber & Faber, 1971)
Edwin Smith and David Renouf	*The Oxford Students Harmony* (O.U.P., 1965)
Paul Steinitz and Stella Sterman	*Harmony in Context* (Belwin-Mills Music, 1974)
Oliver Strunck	*Source Readings in Music History* (Faber & Faber, 1952)
Owen Swindale	*Polyphonic Composition* (O.U.P., 1962)

Index of Composers

Page numbers in Roman type are quotations, in bold type exercises, and those preceded by an asterisk are textual references.

General Index

Page references in bold type indicate main entries.